MW00676939

Basic Education in Rural Pakistan

A Comparative Institutional Analysis of
Government, Private and NGO Schools

Basic Education in Rural Pakistan

A Comparative Institutional Analysis of Government, Private and NGO Schools

SHAHRUKH RAFI KHAN

OXFORD
UNIVERSITY PRESS

OXFORD

UNIVERSITY PRESS

Great Clarendon Street, Oxford OX2 6DP

Oxford University Press is a department of the University of Oxford.
It furthers the University's objective of excellence in research, scholarship,
and education by publishing worldwide in

Oxford New York

Auckland Cape Town Dar es Salaam Hong Kong Karachi
Kuala Lumpur Madrid Melbourne Mexico City Nairobi
New Delhi Shanghai Taipei Toronto

with offices in

Argentina Austria Brazil Chile Czech Republic France Greece
Guatemala Hungary Italy Japan South Korea Poland Portugal
Singapore Switzerland Thailand Turkey Ukraine Vietnam

Oxford is a registered trade mark of Oxford University Press
in the UK and in certain other countries

© Oxford University Press 2005

The moral rights of the author have been asserted

First published 2005

All rights reserved. No part of this publication may be reproduced, translated,
stored in a retrieval system, or transmitted, in any form or by any means,
without the prior permission in writing of Oxford University Press.
Enquiries concerning reproduction should be sent to
Oxford University Press at the address below.

This book is sold subject to the condition that it shall not, by way
of trade or otherwise, be lent, re-sold, hired out or otherwise circulated
without the publisher's prior consent in any form of binding or cover
other than that in which it is published and without a similar condition
including this condition being imposed on the subsequent purchaser.

ISBN-13: 978-0-19-547002-4
ISBN-10: 0-19-547002-8

Typeset in Times & Optima
Printed in Pakistan by
Kagzi Printers, Karachi.
Published by
Ameena Saiyid, Oxford University Press
Plot No. 38, Sector 15, Korangi Industrial Area, PO Box 8214
Karachi-74900, Pakistan.

This book is dedicated to Junita Bunker

Contents

Introduction

The objective of this book on basic rural education is to suggest ways to make the public sector rural primary schooling delivery more effective. The broader objective, and one that would be of more interest to a wider audience in the development community, is to do a comparative institutional analysis of government, private, and NGO schools. We identify processes pushing for improvements in the NGO and private sectors and those resulting in obvious failures in the government sectors. Our focus is on operational lessons derived from NGO and private sector delivery that could make public sector delivery more effective.

It is useful to go back to the inception of the *Human Development Report* (1990, pp. 10-12) to emphasize the importance of education to human development. In defining human development, the Report states '...that it is a process of enlarging people's choices. The more critical ones are, to lead a long and healthy life, to be educated, and to enjoy a decent standard of living.' Thus, education is center stage because knowledge is viewed as essential to the formation of human capabilities and one of the essential elements of human life. Furthermore, the inclusion of adult literacy as one of the three indicators in the quantification of human development is premised on the qualitative improvement of the nature of choices humans make when guided by knowledge.

There is a vast body of research that demonstrates the value of education. Much of this is summarized in World Bank (n.d., pp. 2-3) regarding why investment in education makes sense. This includes its positive impact on economic growth, poverty alleviation, and the fostering of social cohesion and construction of democratic societies. A skilled and productive labor force attracts foreign investment and enhances the spread of new ideas, and technologies. Education also enhances nutrition information and the practice of more healthy behaviors.

Some of the statistics pertaining to female education are particularly notable. Thus, an additional year of schooling reduces child mortality by 10 per cent and reduces total fertility rate by 0.23 births. An increase in one percentage point in the share of women in the population with secondary education is estimated to raise per capita income by 0.3 per cent. Finally, education enhances women's productivity and enables them to participate in the labor force and use more environmentally friendly technologies.

On the individual level, it is one of the main avenues of social mobility and research shows that an additional year of schooling raises earnings by more than 10 per cent in low-income countries. Research has also demonstrated that education raises farm productivity.

Pakistan barely crawled into the group of medium human development countries in 1999, but for 2001, it was ranked third in the low human development country group.[1] The main reason it slipped down and was ranked so low (144/175) was due to its poor performance in education.[2] Its rank based on per capita GDP in purchasing power parity terms was seven points higher than its HDI ranking.[3] For 2002, it reached the top of the low human development countries but remained the only South Asian country ranked in the low human development category—all the rest including Bangladesh, Bhutan, India and Nepal had attained medium human development status, and education continued to be the cause of this lagging performance for Pakistan.[4]

Since its birth in 1947, Pakistan has attained an adult illiteracy rate of 41.5 per cent that is even below the average of 52.7 per cent for the least developed countries.[5] Its net primary enrollment rate of 66 per cent was again lower than the average of 79 per cent for South Asia or 74 per cent for low-income countries respectively.[6]

Pakistan's performance in closing the gender gap has been equally poor. The ratio of boys to girls at the primary, secondary, and tertiary levels in 2001 was 55, 63, and 38 per cent respectively.[7] Its total and female gross primary enrollment rate in 1995 was 74 per cent and 45 per cent compared to an average of 101 per cent and 87 per cent respectively for all developing countries.[8]

The ratio of literate females to males (15:24) increased from 49 per cent in 1990 to 60 per cent in 2001, but remained well below the 85 per cent for low-income countries in 2001.[9] Overall female to male literacy ratio in 2002 (15 and above) was 53 per cent compared to 70 per cent for low-income countries.[10]

The commitment to education can be gauged from expenditure on education as a percentage of GDP and this declined from 2.6 per cent in 1990 to 1.8 per cent between 1999 and 2001, and further down to

1.7 per cent by 2002–2003.[11] While educational expenditure is important, effective schooling models will not succeed unless there is a strong desire for education.

The linking within the human capital model of investment in education with the economic returns to education has, in the Pakistani context, led to a flawed communications strategy. There are important reasons for socially and individually investing in education. From society's point of view, the attainment of human development, enlightenment, and nation-building are some of the worthy objectives. From the individual point of view, at a minimum, socialization and broadening horizons are easily attainable, but instrumental advantages such as reading newspapers, medical indicators, and negotiating government forms are also achieved. However, the link established by the human capital model of education with economic returns, in the form of a promise of better jobs, has resulted in the onset of disillusionment and despair.[12] In view of the fact that the labor market is not universally fair and competitive, and given the very high unemployment rates in many occupational categories, people's personal experience shows that education is not necessarily leading to better jobs. This has led to disenchantment with education among many poor families. Thus, the communication strategy for popularizing basic education or universalizing education should de-link education from the economic motives and highlight the other numerous reasons for pursuing it.

The problem that motivated our concern with basic education is manifold. First, Pakistan's poor performance in the international context reported on above provides powerful motivation. Second, despite the Social Action Plan (SAP), data shows that the net enrollment rates for girls declined between 1991 and 1996–97 from 31 to 30. They subsequently picked up and reached 33 per cent by 2001–2002, which is also very low.[13] For rural boys, the drop in net enrollment rate was greater, i.e. from 50 to 43 between 1991 and 1996–97 they stayed at this low level till 2001–2002.[14] The declines were even sharper for the most vulnerable categories such as rural girls in the bottom income quintile of the population, and by 2001–2002 the enrollment rate for rural girls in the lowest income quintile at 22 per cent was less than half that for the upper income quintile at 53 per cent.

Third, there has been a massive exodus from government to non-government (private and NGO) schools over the last decade of the twentieth century. Thus, between 1991 and 1995–96, absolute enrollment growth rates in the non-government sector were 61 per cent and 131 per cent for girls and boys respectively. By 2001–2002, rural primary boys and girls enrollment in government schools for the upper income quintile was 64 and 69 per cent as a percentage of total primary enrollments. By contrast, these numbers were respectively 92 and 90 per cent for the lowest income quintile.

Finally, non-government schools out-perform government schools by a large margin in all the standard, crude quality indicators such as student-teacher ratios and class size, and in basic facilities such as percentages providing classrooms, desks, water, and electricity.

Given the above, the focus of this book is on rural public schooling at the primary level.[15] The focus on schooling is necessary because we view basic education as a human right and necessary for a more prosperous and just society. The focus on public sector schooling is justified because we continue to see education as primarily the state's responsibility and, despite the move towards non-government schooling, as indicated above, the public sector still accounted for over 90 per cent of total provision of schooling in rural areas for the poor in 2001–2002.[16] Since education is one of the only legal means of social mobility, we feel public education, that serves the poor, needs to be improved if 'evening the odds', or equity is an important social objective. In addition, public education needs to be improved because it establishes a standard.

If rural public schooling is of very poor quality, non-government schooling does not have to be much better to draw children away from it. We found that even some poor households stretch their resources to enroll their children in non-government schools (refer to chapter 2). However, the exodus of children of the better-off families from public schools creates a vicious cycle. The more well-off families represent an important constituency for maintaining standards since they have an effective 'voice'. Once they 'exit', the countervailing power needed to maintain standards in public schooling is no longer present and quality deteriorates further.[17]

Using Government of Pakistan (2001a, pp. 31, 38, 61) and Government of Pakistan, Statistical Appendix, (2001b, p. 129), we determined that for 1999–2000, 9.1 per cent of total primary schools (grades 1-5) and 68.2 per cent middle schools (grades 6-8) respectively were non-government establishments. Of these, 48 per cent and 41 per cent respectively were rural. Since there may or may not be primary sections in middle schools and since urban and rural class sizes vary a great deal, a more accurate contribution of the 'non-government' sector to total schooling can be gauged by its contribution to total enrollments. In this regard, 22 per cent and 19 per cent of total primary and middle enrollments respectively were due to the 'non-government' sector, a sizable contribution by any standard. Of these 'non-government' sector enrollments, 34 per cent and 27 per cent respectively were in rural areas.

'Non-government' is implicitly defined above by the Government of Pakistan (2001a, p. 61) to include privately owned, NGO, trust, foundation and other schools. Since there is no definition provided of an NGO school, one could argue that all non-government, non-privately owned schools could be classified as NGO schools. Using this broad definition, 20 per cent of total private schooling is non-commercial while 7 per cent of total 'non-government' schools classify as NGO schools if a narrow definition, based on registration as non-profit, is used.

While rural communities are often unable to distinguish between NGO and private schools, they are in fact very distinct entities. To begin with, the registering bodies for a commercial venture and a non-profit organization are completely different and therefore their charters, and hence their aims, objectives, and missions are also different. The private schools are no different from profit entities anywhere else, and, to the extent that they want to maximize profits over time, they have to be responsive to their clients (parents).

A mission for both enhancing education, but also reshaping society in their particular vision drives the NGO schools. In this regard, the mission statements of overtly religious NGOs and a more secular NGO are vastly different. Essentially, both these organizations deliver good basic education, but the orientation and the composition of boards of governors to whom they report are vastly different.

This also highlights another important distinction between private and NGO schools in the rural context. While there are chains of private sector schools across urban Pakistan, the private sector schools in rural Pakistan are generally of the 'one-off' owner-operated type. However, given that these schools have caught on and met with an unexpected positive response among parents who have lost faith in government education, entrepreneurs who are not educationists themselves fund such schools and hire principals/managers to run them for profit. By contrast, most effective NGO schools are run by multiple-school NGOs rather than one-off NGOs, although we included seven of the latter variety in our sample. Having determined the quantitative significance of NGO and private schools and how they differ from government schools, we now turn to a brief synopsis of the book chapters.

The first chapter is an overview of the state of basic education and is based on secondary data. The other five chapters draw on primary data generated by a survey of 129 government, NGO, and private schools (forty-three each). The research design and sampling are described in Appendix 1 and the instruments used for data collection are included as Appendix 2. A paired sampling methodology was used by which we first randomly tracked forty-three NGO schools and then identified forty-three of the nearest private and government schools. This provided a very small sample of government schools, which are our major concern. However, given that formal NGO schools are a 'rare population' and given our interest in a comparative evaluation, we proceeded with this design on the basis of advice from a sampling expert. However, the reader is cautioned about the small sample of government schools and should bear in mind the emphasis on the comparative review. We, nonetheless, have confidence in our findings about government schooling because they are consistent with the broader literature on basic education in Pakistan.

As indicated above, in chapter 1 we present an overview of basic education. Educational expenditure as a percentage of GDP was protected over the first phase of SAP (1993–1996) and increased by about 0.2 per cent of GDP. However, despite SAP protection, it declined to the pre-SAP level for 1998–99, and by 2002–2003 declined to 1.7 per cent as a percentage of GDP compared to the SAP peak of 2.5 per cent in 1995–96. While there is evidence that, in some respects, the gender and regional gaps closed, the poorest continued to be excluded from schooling, the rural female income gap in schooling widened, and, if the poor did attend, they were the most likely to drop out. Also, net rural primary enrollment rates for boys actually declined over the SAP periods and they were virtually unchanged for girls.

Chapter 2 is the core chapter of the book. We use a principal-agent framework to compare the institutional effectiveness of rural, primary schooling delivery of the government with the NGO and private sectors using qualitative analysis. Our main findings are that NGO schools were the most successful in many respects and that 'good management' and/or 'good leadership' were the key ingredient for sound schooling.

In chapter 3, we explore parent-teacher associations or school management committees (PTAs/SMCs) that are an important way of realizing collective action and participation in schooling. Field visits, a literature search, and the sample survey were the three sources used to explore the status of PTAs/SMCs that have been established by the government and NGO sectors. Our main finding is that public sector reform, to alter the power relation between parents, teachers and government officials, are needed to make participation effective in schooling. In general, NGO schools performed only marginally better than government schools in engendering participation.

Given how influential the World Bank is in the development field and given the structural changes it brings about in most borrowing countries in most sectors, it is important to examine its policies carefully. We use the education sector in Pakistan as a case study for this purpose in chapter 4 and conceptually examine several World Bank endorsed or maintained hypotheses. We state conceptual reservations on important policy initiatives that have been implemented and/or are being endorsed. We present a quantitative analysis of some of these hypotheses using classes (average class performance) as a unit of analysis in a comparative context.

In chapter 5, the effectiveness of the different school types is also explored using students rather than classes as the unit of analysis. This chapter uses a production function approach to identify the impact of student, parent, teacher, and school policy variables on student cognitive skill test scores. It also evaluates the importance of 'intangibles' based on field observation. In addition, it explores the impact on cognitive skills of cost cutting and other school policy measures. These empirical exercises are again conducted in a comparative institutional context that includes government, private, and NGO schools.

Public sector salaries, including those that apply to rural teachers in Pakistan, are rigidly determined by educational qualifications and experience. If it can be determined that educational qualifications and experience enhance teacher cognitive skills, which in turn enhance student cognitive skills, one can infer that there is some rationality to such a salary structure and that teacher incentives are compatible with teacher effectiveness. We utilized two sets of data to test these propositions in chapter 6. The first, based only on a survey of government schools, seemed to suggest that some rationality, with many qualifications, existed in rural public sector schooling salary scales. However, utilizing the more recent comparative data set described above showed no such rationality existed in the public sector while salaries were responsive to qualifications in the non-government and private sectors.

The introduction and the first three chapters of the book as well as the concluding chapter have been written to be accessible to the general reader. While chapters 4-6 require some familiarity with statistical analysis, the slightly technical material and statistical tables have been relegated to endnotes and annexes and only the results have been reported in the text and made accessible to the general reader.

Most of the research for this book was done at the Sustainable Development Policy Institute (SDPI), Islamabad between 1998 and 2002. The Asia Foundation (TAF) funded the research as part of its Basic Education Project that included researchers from the SDPI and the London School of Economics. My appreciation to Eric Jensen who headed The Asia Foundation in Pakistan when the project was conceived in 1998 and who was extremely supportive, interacted with us, but allowed us complete freedom to pursue the research as the project evolved. Thanks are also due to Mehnaz Aziz who was the program officer in education at The Asia Foundation during the project period. The work was completed as a visiting faculty member at the University of Utah and Mount Holyoke College. Thus, I am indebted to all four institutions.

I am grateful to Haris Gazdar for initiating this project and, as a partner in the project along with Tahir Andrabi, for having conducted a very interesting and independent analysis.[18] He also provided very useful feedback on earlier versions of several of the chapters of this book. Thanks are due to Sajid Kazmi who provided research assistance on several of the chapters, co-authored the report chapter 2 is based on, and very ably led the fieldwork. Zainab Latif was meticulous, demanding, and the soul of the field teams for much of the fieldwork and also a co-author of the report chapter 2 is based on. Fareeha Zafar was instrumental in getting me involved in a study on school management committees/parent-teacher associations and wrote a report with me that was supported by NORAD (Norwegian Agency for Development Corporation). This became the basis for chapter 3 and thanks are due to Hazel Bines for providing valuable comments on this work and for encouraging further work on the issue. The research for chapter 6 was built on earlier work done with Jere Behrman, David Ross and Richard Sabot as part of the USAID/IFPRI (United States Agency for International Development/International Food Policy Research Institute) Human Capital Accumulation in Post-Green

Revolution Pakistan Project and, as such, their contribution is gratefully acknowledged. Thanks are due to Sohail Malik for getting me involved in the IFPRI project and therefore for getting me to resume work on education. Comments from Lubna Chaudhry on an early draft of chapter 6 are gratefully acknowledged. Thanks are also due to Shahnaz Kazi for providing research material on several occasions. Since much of the work in this book has gone through the journal refereeing process, the anonymous comments of referees contributed to the work and, as the author, I bear responsibility for the remaining errors.

This book could never even have been attempted were it not for the very diligent fieldwork of a very able group of post-graduates. Their field reports provided many useful insights that were the basis of the core chapter (chapter 2) of the book. Thus, thanks are due to Abida Muneer, Noreen Lehri, and Samina Raisani for their work in Balochistan; Saiqa Bibi, Uzma Qazi, and Amna Khan for their work in the NWFP; Amjad Iqbal, Shabaz Bokhari, Saadia Almas, and Rahat Jabeen for their work in the Punjab; and Abdur Rashid Memon, Saira Memon, Sanam Memon, and Rehana Shahani Baloch for their work in Sindh. Finally, I would like to thank the reviewers and editors of Oxford University Press, Pakistan. Most research is in many ways a collective effort and this is certainly true for this book.

References

Gazdar, H., 1999, 'Universal Basic Education in Pakistan: Commentary on Strategy and Results of a Survey', SDPI Working Paper Series No. 39, Islamabad.

Government of Pakistan, 1998, 'Education Sector Performance in the 1990s: Analysis from the PIHS', Federal Bureau of Statistics, Islamabad.

Government of Pakistan, 1999, 2001a, 2004, *Economic Survey*, Federal Bureau of Statistics, Islamabad.

Government of Pakistan, 2001b, *Census of Private Educational Institutions in Pakistan*, Federal Bureau of Statistics, Statistics Division, Islamabad, 2001.

Government of Pakistan, 2003a, *Pakistan Integrated Household Survey 2001-2002*, Federal Bureau of Statistics, Islamabad.

Hirschman, A. O., 1970, *Exit, Voice and Loyalty: Responses to Declines in Firms, Organizations, and States* (Cambridge, Massachusetts: Harvard University Press).

Khan, S. R., 2003, Khan, S. R., 2004, *Pakistan under Musharraf (1999–2002): Economic and Political Reforms* (Lahore, Pakistan: Vanguard Press).

RSPN (Rural Support Program Network), 2003, 'Including the Poor in the PRSP Process', PRSP Consultations Nov. 2002–Feb. 2003, Islamabad, Pakistan.

UNDP, 1990, 1998, 1999, 2002, 2003, 2004, *Human Development Report* (New York: Oxford University Press).

World Bank, n.d., 'Opening Doors: Education and the World Bank', Human Development Network, The World Bank, Washington, DC.

NOTES

1. UNDP (1999, p. 136) and (2003, p. 239).
2. UNDP (2003, p. 239).
3. Ibid. Per capita GDP in purchasing power parity terms controls for the differences in the cost of living across countries.
4. UNDP (2004, pp. 140-1)
5. UNDP (2004, pp. 141-2).
6. UNDP (2003, pp. 199, 202).
7. UNDP (2003, pp. 204, 207).
8. UNDP (1998, p. 163).
9. Ibid.
10. UNDP (2004, pp. 227-8).
11. UNDP (2003, p. 268) and Government of Pakistan (2004), Statistical Appendix, p. 7. For more details on expenditure on education see chapter 1, section 1.3.
12. One of the best brief accounts of this is the documentation by Rural Support Program Network (2003) of the voices of the poor as part of the consultations for Pakistan's Interim-Poverty Reduction Strategy Paper. Refer to RSPN (2003).
13. Government of Pakistan (1998, 2003a). These are also the sources for the information in the next two paragraphs.
14. Gross primary enrollment rate is defined as the number of children attending primary schools (classes 1-5) divided by the number of children (aged 5-9) multiplied by 100. For net enrollment rate the denominator is the same but the numerator is the number of children aged 5-9 attending the primary level. Thus, net enrollment rates are always lower than gross enrollment rates. In both cases, children attending *katchi* (generally children less than 5 years accompanying older siblings to school and sitting in class 1 but not formally enrolled) were excluded.
15. Basic education is at times defined to include the middle level (classes 6 to 8).
16. Non-government includes both private and NGO schools unless otherwise specified. We prefer the term PIO (public interest organization) to NGO, but given the common reference to the latter, that term is used. For a case for using PIO refer to Khan (2004).
17. Hirschman (1970) first used the terms 'voice' and 'exit'.
18. The first draft of this companion work was published as Gazdar (1999).

1 [1]

An Overview of Basic Education

1.1. Introduction

The justified fear of austerity imposed by structural adjustment is that the social sectors, including education, are likely to face the first and major budget cuts. This fear was based on the experience in several developing countries and this led to an important critique by Cornia, Jolly, and Stewart (1987) who urged, as per the title of their book, *Adjustment With a Human Face*. An important finding of their analysis was that structural adjustment was associated with the neglect of the social sectors and the poor, and thus their main recommendation was reversing this neglect.

In Pakistan, the World Bank's (Bank) effort to put a human face on structural adjustment came in the form of the Social Action Program (SAP). The bulk of SAP funding was that of the Government (see below) and one stated concern was redressing the poor performance of the social sectors relative to the economic sectors and relative to a reference group of developing countries. Other stated objectives of SAP included improving efficiency, quality, and closing the regional, gender, and income gaps in educational access and attainment.[2]

The social services targeted by SAP include basic education, primary health, population and welfare, and rural water supply and sanitation.[3] Within the context of this program, the first Social Action Program Project (SAPP-I), with partial donor support, had a three year duration from 1993–1996 with a total expenditure of Rs 103.6 billion, the bulk of it provided by the Government of Pakistan. Under the auspices of SAPP-I, between 1993 and 1996, 15,487 new primary schools were planned and 13,356 actually built. In addition to these, 6319 new classrooms were built and 5794 buildings built for shelterless schools. SAPP-II (1996–2000) was launched with an estimated expenditure of Rs 498.8 billion (of which 65 per cent was allocated to basic schooling) with about 80 per cent domestic contribution. This represented a substantial increase in real terms.[4] SAP was extensively reviewed and discontinued due to allegations of widespread corruption and misuse of funds.

The main purpose of this chapter is to review secondary data to ascertain the extent to which Pakistan attained its objectives in the education sector via SAP or otherwise. In the second section, we discuss SAP in a broader conceptual context and briefly describe the secondary data used for this chapter. In the third section, we review the educational expenditure patterns under SAP. In the fourth section, we more directly review the attainment of various SAP objectives. In the fifth section, we show that the failure of government schooling has resulted in a phenomenal expansion in non-government schooling.[5] We end with a concluding section.

1.2. Conceptual context and data

The World Bank viewed SAP as part of a poverty strategy that had two planks. The first to enhance growth, and the second to invest in human capital to enable people to respond as new opportunities emerge.[6] To elaborate, the two-pronged approach to poverty alleviation was first to ensure that there was economic growth, which is assumed to create jobs, and second to ensure that the poor were contenders for these jobs, since human capital investments in them are designed to make them more productive.

Thus, the SAP project was designed explicitly to reduce poverty and misery by improving human capital access for the poor. One could argue that investments in human capital, to ensure that the poor become better market players, is a long-run, hands-off approach to poverty alleviation. First, it aims to eliminate poverty among future generations and thus ignores the current poor. Second, even if poor households are reached by SAP-like initiatives, given the high unemployment rates and various social and institutional distortions, there is no guarantee they will find jobs even if they are more productive.[7] Therefore, central to a sensible poverty strategy must be the creation of sustainable livelihoods.[8]

During the SAP period, The Federal Bureau of Statistics, Pakistan (FBS) started conducting annual surveys called the Pakistan Integrated Household Surveys (PIHS). The stated objective was to provide 'household and community level data which can be used to monitor, evaluate and assess the impact of the Social Action Program'. The FBS presents reports based on data collected from large national data sets. The *Round 2, 1996-97* (n.d.) report was prepared within an impressive two months of the completion of the data collection process of a survey of 12,622 households. Not only has the FBS demonstrated efficiency with regards to regular data collection, it also issues reports that contain a wealth of data in tabular form and some basic reporting. All the relevant sampling and data collection information is carefully reported. PIHS 2001–2002, following in the same tradition, was based on a survey of 16,182 households. For those wishing to probe further, the primary data for all the years are easily accessible on diskette and on the FBS website. This chapter is based on the tables reported in the PIHS 1996-97 and PIHS 2000–2001 and other secondary government data available in statistical reports.

1.3. Educational expenditure patterns and outputs

As indicated earlier, the Social Action Program (SAP) was designed to protect the social sectors. It is, however, possible that while expenditures on elementary education increase, those to other levels of education decrease. In that case, SAP expenditures would not represent an addition in educational expenditures but merely a restructuring. We present the total allocations to the education sector as a percentage of GDP in Table 1.1 below.

Table 1.1 Expenditure on education as a percentage of GDP

Year/Expenditure	Education expenditure as a percentage of GDP
1988-89	2.4
1989-90	2.2
1990-91	2.1
1991-92	2.2
1992-93	2.2
1993-94	2.2
1994-95	2.4
1995-96	2.4
1996-97	2.5
1997-98	2.3
1998-99	2.2
1999-00	2.1
2000-01	1.6
2001-02	1.9
2002-03	1.7

Source: Government of Pakistan (2004), Statistical Appendix, p. 7.

Table 1.1 above reports information on educational expenditures from 1988-89 onwards, which could be considered the first fiscal year of the intensive phase of structural adjustment for Pakistan. The first fiscal year reflecting SAP expenditures is 1993-94. Between these two years, total educational expenditures as a percentage of GDP declined, but subsequently picked up and there is a 0.2 per cent increase between the benchmark SAP year and 1996, the final year of SAPP-I. However, educational expenditure subsequently declined to the pre-SAPP-I level despite SAPP-II protection. Post SAP (2000), educational expenditures declined even below the pre-SAP levels.

Another way of looking at the expenditures is by comparing them with the allocations. For almost all the Five-Year Plan periods, expenditures generally fell far short of the allocations at the primary level as shown below in Table 1.2.

Table 1.2 Ratio of expenditures to allocations across the plan periods

Plan periods/Level	Primary	Non-primary
First Plan (1955-60)	41.2	69.7
Second Plan (1960-65)	24.1	104.4
Third Plan (1965-70)	36.7	50.9
Non-Plan period (1970-78)	93.6	89.4
Fifth Plan (1978-83)	46.7	55.2
Sixth Plan (1983-88)	45.3	113.6
Seventh Plan (1988-93)	63.1	110.2
Eighth Plan (1993-98)	47.7	38.2
Ninth Plan (1998–2003)	20.4	35.0

Source: Based on Government of Pakistan/UNICEF (2002, pp. 36-8).

Except for in the non-Plan period, expenditures exceeded half of allocations for the primary level only twice and in the Ninth Plan period dropped to a fifth of allocations, thus confirming fears of social observers that primary education is the primary candidate for austerity cuts. In the rest of the education sector, expenditures actually exceeded total allocations overall in three of the nine periods indicated in Table 1.2, although even here expenditures to allocation ratios were very low between 1993 and 2003.

Aggregate numbers can mask many interesting details, and so it is useful to probe deeper to see how the expenditures cited above translated into a change over time in basic facilities for the primary and middle levels. Unfortunately, the data does not allow probing in much depth but, again, at an aggregate level, it is possible to see the changes in the student-institution, student-teacher, and teacher-institution ratios over time in Table 1.3 below.

Table 1.3 Student-institution, student-teacher, and teacher-institution ratios by gender, level and time

Time	Student-institution ratio				Teacher-institution ratio		Student-teacher ratio	
	Primary		Middle		Primary	Middle	Primary	Middle
	Girls	Boys	Girls	Boys				
1990-91	118.2	86.3	247.6	373.4	2.4	9.7	39.0	33.5
1991-92	117.5	86.9	245.1	386.0	2.6	9.7	36.6	34.1
1992-93	120.6	87.9	194.9	305.4	2.3	6.1	42.6	42.3
1993-94	126.4	87.5	216.0	316.2	2.4	6.6	41.3	41.1
1994-95	134.2	88.4	240.5	352.7	2.4	6.9	42.7	44.1
1995-96	131.4	88.5	222.8	307.2	2.3	7.1	43.9	38.2
1996-97	146.6	85.9	238.1	272.3	2.2	5.8	47.7	44.0
1997-98	137.2	95.8	212.8	245.1	2.2	5.1	50.2	45.6
1998-99	114.2	114.0	198.3	248.7	2.3	5.0	50.6	45.7
1999-00	120.2	116.6	199.4	242.4	2.3	5.0	52.3	44.9
2000-01	148.8	102.5	184.4	227.5	2.0	5.3	58.1	39.3
2001-02 (P)	149.8	105.2	184.7	228.1	2.0	5.3	58.3	39.4

Source: Government of Pakistan (2004), Statistical Appendix (pp. 89-90).
Notes: P = Provisional
Student-teacher and teacher-institution ratios are not reported by gender because while data in all sources report female and male teachers, they do not indicate the number of female teachers teaching in 'all boys' schools. Thus, the ratios would be understated for boy's schools and overstated for girl's schools if we assume all female teachers only teach in girl's schools.

One could view all these ratios as very crude indicators of quality in so far as lower ratios indicate less crowding on an aggregate level. Student-institution ratios rose for both boys and girls since 1990-91 at the primary level, and more sharply for girls than boys. The ratios however steadily declined for both genders at the middle level. Of greater concern is the steady decline in the number of teachers per institution at both the primary and middle levels. Student-teacher ratios rose for both levels, but much more sharply for the primary level. Such a rise accords with Bank research suggesting that ratios can be as high as 45:1 without impairing teaching efficiency.[9] While the average boy ratio of 39:1 for the middle level in 2001-02 was below this threshold, the average ratio of 58:1 at the primary level should again be cause for concern. We revisit the quality and crowding issue in section 1.4.3. and turn now to a more direct review of the attainment of SAP objectives.

1.4. Assessing the Social Action Program objectives[10]

1.4.1. Closing the age, gender and regional gaps

The data on population that has 'ever attended school' by age for 2001–2002 shows that there was a strong demand for schooling. Overall, 80 per cent of the boys and 59 per cent of the girls in the 10-14 'age cohort' had attended school at some point (85 per cent and 83 per cent respectively in urban areas). Thus, the potential to raise educational attainment by providing quality schooling was high.

There was also a strong inverse association of school attendance with age and this association became more prominent over time. Thus, school attendance for the younger cohorts was much higher (80 per cent for the 10-14 age group compared to 31 per cent for the 60 plus age group). More important, the progress among females and rural areas for the younger cohorts is notable. Male and female enrollment in the 10-14 'age cohort' was 85 per cent and 83 per cent respectively compared to 51 per cent and 12 per cent respectively for the 60 plus 'age cohort'. Similarly, the total urban and rural enrollments were 84 per cent and 65 per cent respectively in the 10-14 'age cohort' compared to 34 per cent and 14 per cent respectively in the 60 plus cohort. Thus, while in absolute terms the percentages need to be higher, the age differential and the closing of the gender gaps are encouraging. These trends are also evident from data on primary school 'completers'.

The above analysis pertains to progress over a time period that began much before but includes the SAP period. There is no discontinuity as such observable in the data. There is, however, an interesting additional finding over the first SAP period evident from juxtaposing the percentages in the youngest cohort that 'ever attended school' with an older cohort who 'completed the primary level' some years later. In 1991, 84 per cent boys and 53 per cent girls in the 10-14 'age cohort' had ever attended school. This is roughly the cohort that would be in the 15-19 'age cohort' in 1995-96. In the latter year, 71 per cent boys and 44 per cent girls were reported as completing the primary level in the 15-19 'age cohort'.

This finding is interesting for several reasons. First, it shows that the implied dropout rate was much lower than the mythical 50 per cent that is frequently cited in the press and even scholarly publications.[11] Second, the implied dropout rate seems to be lower for girls. It was possible to investigate this issue more directly by looking at data on primary school 'non-completers' among the 10-18 'age cohort' and the data on dropout rates for 2001–2002. Non-completion of 8 per cent among girls was lower than 13 per cent non-completion for boys in the urban areas. However, in rural areas, the non-completion for girls of 20 per cent was higher than the 16 per cent non-completion for boys. However, it is still much less than the generally stated overall 50 per cent non-completion. While dropout rates for both male and female increase by class at the primary level, they peak at about 12.6 per cent in the transition from class 4 to class 5. The dropout rate of 28 per cent between classes 5 and 6 is higher since this is the time many parents decide to withdraw their children from school mainly due to the high direct and indirect expense involved or because they prefer to not have girls attend school after they reach puberty.[12]

While there were some SAP successes, there were also significant failures. Between 1991 and 1996-97, the net rural primary enrollment rate for boys declined from 50 per cent to 43 per cent and that for girls declined from 31 per cent to 30 per cent. Over the same period, urban boy and girl net primary enrollments declined from 61 per cent to 56 per cent and from 57 per cent to 55 per cent respectively.[13] Since improving rural enrollments in general, and those of girls specifically, was identified as a major SAP objective, this is a glaring shortcoming. Also, the regional gap for boys became larger and net girl enrollment rate actually declined in the rural areas at the primary level. This failing is actually understated since the net rural enrollment rates reported include non-government schooling. Net enrollment rates (including *kacchi* [pre-school]) were still only 53 per cent and 44 per cent overall for boys and girls respectively by 2001–2002.

1.4.2. Closing the income gap

Closing the income gap in educational attainment was another major SAP objective. In all provinces, gross and net primary enrollment rates varied positively with the level of income in both rural and urban areas for both genders and at both the primary and middle levels.[14] To give an example, the rural primary level net enrollment rate for the upper quintile in the Punjab, the most prosperous province, was 77 and 69 for boys and girls respectively while it was 41 and 28 respectively for the lowest quintile.[15] Again, across the board, a much higher percentage of children belonging to households in the lowest quintile never attended school or dropped out if they did attend.[16]

To get a sense of how educational attainment changed over the SAP years for girls in the lowest income group, we looked at gross enrollment rates for girls across the five quintiles between 1991, 1995-96, and 2001–2002 and these are reported below in Table 1.4.

Table 1.4. Gross primary enrolment rates for girls for 1991, 1995-96, and 2001–2002 by income group.

Quintile/Year	1991		1995-96		2001–2002	
	Urban	Rural	Urban	Rural	Urban	Rural
Ist. Quintile	77	27	67	35	56	34
2nd. Quintile	78	39	82	49	67	47
3rd. Quintile	89	53	100	60	84	56
4th. Quintile	101	70	107	63	102	66
5th. Quintile	100	64	113	84	110	81

Source: Primary data analysis based on the PIHS 1991 and PIHS 1995-96[17] and PIHS 2001–2002 (2002, p. 36).

Girl's enrollment in urban areas for the lowest income category dropped across the decade while that for the second and third lowest quintile first rose and then dropped again. In rural areas, for the lowest income groups, there was an increase during the first phase of SAP, but no further gains in the second SAP period. While one could argue that the first phase of SAP had a positive impact on gross rural female girl enrollments in the lowest income group, the gross enrollment gap between the lowest and highest rural girls' quintiles increased dramatically from 37 percentage points in 1991 to 49 percentage points in 1995-96 and from 31 percentage points to 46 percentage points for all girls during this period. These gaps in enrollment rates in rural areas and overall (urban and rural) increased to 52 per cent and 50 per cent respectively for 2001–2002.

In responding to questions why children had 'never attended school' or 'not completed primary school', the most frequent household answer in 1995-96 was that schooling was too expensive. Thus for non-completion, 35 per cent of the parents mentioned this to be a reason for girls and 29 per cent mentioned it to be a reason for boys in urban areas. These percentages were 19 and 20 per cent respectively for rural areas. The other important related reason cited was that the children were needed to help at home or at work. Ten per cent and 21 per cent parents of boys in urban and rural areas respectively and 9 per cent and 19 per cent respectively of parents of girls mentioned this.[18] In 2001–2002, expense continued to be the pre-dominant reason for children not completing or never attending school for both boys and girls, and in both urban and rural areas.

If the government wants to reach the poor and improve the overall educational attainment, a proactive approach would have to be used. At the moment, many poor children are either not attending or dropping out if they do attend. A more proactive approach would include tuition waivers, free uniforms, books and other supplies for the poorest.[19] Identifying the poorest would have to be the task of the school management committees (SMCs) that only include teachers and parents of children currently in school. [20] Including local notables, as currently done, is meaningless since they have a very limited legitimate stake in the school and can easily subvert expenditure targeting.[21]

The public-private divide is 'as expected' much more stark by income group. Thus, by 2001–2002, over 90 per cent of the girls and boys from the lowest income group (lowest quintile) attended government schools in rural areas compared to only about a third in the upper income group (highest quintile). In urban areas, about three-quarters and a quarter of children of the lower and upper income groups respectively attended government schools. Thus, another significant SAP shortcoming pertains to the inability of the education system to reach the poorest.

1.4.3. Quality

Retention would also be more likely if the quality of public sector schooling improved. While expenditure on schooling is a very crude measure of quality, other things being equal, it can provide some information. In 1996-97, excluding fees, expenditures on uniforms (which are roughly identical), books and supplies, private tuition, transport and other education related expenditure per pupil in private urban primary schools at Rs 1520 was almost double the per pupil expenditure of Rs 851 in government urban primary schools. There was a similar differential in rural areas (Rs 1229 as opposed to Rs 670).[22]

One could use the non-government sector as a benchmark to ascertain how the government sector was performing in 1996-97 on selected quality indicators as reported below in Table 1.5.

Table 1.5. Selected quality indicators by type of school and region.

Regional	Urban		Rural	
Type of school	G	NG	G	NG
SIR	232	165	96	117
SCR	41	25	40	28
STR	24	18	29	24
Percentage teaching in classroom	77	97	55	82
Percentage schools that provide desks to students	56	92	17	70
Percentage schools with water supply	56	92	17	70
Percentage schools with electricity	76	98	27	88
Women teachers as percentage of total	46	85	36	71

Source: Government of Pakistan (1998, pp. 66-7).
Notes: The results are based on a survey of 1227 government and 311 non-government primary schools conducted in 1995-96.
    G: Government
    NG: Non-government
    SIR: Student-institution ratio
    SCR: Student-classroom ratio
    STR: Student-teacher ratio

If the non-government sector is used as a benchmark, the government sector needs to improve its supply side indicators. For example, only 55 per cent of rural government primary teaching occured in a classroom compared to 82 per cent for non-government schools; 17 per cent of government schools provided desks to students compared to 70 per cent of non-government schools; 17 per cent of government schools had water supply compared to 71 per cent for non-government schools; 27 per cent of government schools had electricity compared to 88 per cent for non-government schools.

More recent data on public sector school facilities does not suggest much improvement in the public sector. Statistics on facilities compiled by the Academy of Educational Planning and Management (Government of Pakistan, 2003a, pp. 47-62) indicate that 70 per cent of rural primary schools still had no electricity, 46 per cent had no water, 69 per cent had no latrine, and 65 per cent were without a boundary wall.

Also, the sample data reported above reinforces the concern about congestion raised by the aggregate data reported in Table 1.3. The student-classroom ratio of 40 and 41 in government urban and rural primary schools is high. However, the student-teacher ratio of 24 and 29 respectively is more reasonable. Data from another source (census rather than a sample) that allows a computation of these ratios by region, school type, and level are reported below in Table 1.6.

Table 1.6 Student-teacher, student-institution, and teacher-institution ratios by region, school level, and type (2000–2001)

Level	Student-teacher ratio		Student-institution ratio		Teacher-institution ratio	
	G	NG	G	NG	G	NG
Primary						
Urban	34.5	63.9	207.1	395.7	6.0	6.2
Rural	36.5	54.1	78.3	217.8	2.1	4.0
Middle						
Urban	75.2	9.4	511.3	86.7	6.8	9.2
Rural	17.6	6.3	130.1	47.0	7.4	7.4

Source: Based on Government of Pakistan (2003a, pp. 3-5).
Notes: G: Government
         NG: Non-Government

These student-teacher ratios at the primary level for the government sector for both urban and rural schools are also shown to be reasonable by this data source. The problem area was a high level of congestion in government urban middle schools as accounted for by the high student-teacher ratios (75) and student-institution ratios (511). The high student-teacher ratios in non-government schools at the primary level probably resulted from the very rapid enrollment growth in such schools that we report in the next section. The information content of the other ratios mirror these results with the most notable finding being the low teacher-institution ratio of 2.1 for rural government primary schools which was half that of the comparable non-government schools.

The crude quality indicators in Table 1.6 and supporting information reinforce the qualitative analysis reported in chapter 2 and both suggest a fundamental failure in government schooling. The result is a massive move away from government schooling at both the primary and middle levels as shown in the next section.

1.5. Growth of non-government schooling

Table 1.7 below reports on the relative growth of absolute primary enrollments in government and non-government schools.

Table 1.7. Estimated enrollments and enrollments growth at the primary level by type of school and gender

(Millions)

	1991		1995-96		Percentage growth	
	Girls	Boys	Girls	Boys	Girls	Boys
Govt.	2.63	5.00	3.23	5.18	23.2	3.6
Non-Govt.	0.20	0.26	0.32	0.59	60.50	130.90

Source: Based on Government of Pakistan (1998, p. 23).

First, since it is possible for absolute enrollments (numerator) growth to be positive while the net enrollment growth rate is negative (refer to Note 13), the numbers in Table 1.7 do not contradict the numbers reported in section 1.4 indicating the decline in net enrollment rates. Second, non-government enrollments grew far more rapidly than government sector enrollments, particularly for boys. Third, while non-government enrollments at 11 per cent for boys and 10 per cent for girls in 1995-96 still represent a small fraction of total enrollments, the trend showed that non-government enrollments were growing rapidly. Finally, this rapid growth rate in non-government enrollments understates the poor growth performance of government sector net enrollment rates because the data for public and private performance are reported in aggregate form. The trend reported in Table 1.7 continued into the rest of the decade as shown below in Table 1.8.

Table 1.8. Ratio of non-government schools to total enrollments and institutions by region, school level, gender, and type (2000–2001)

Level	Enrollments				Institutions	
	Urban		Rural		Urban	Rural
	Boys		Girls		Boys	Girls
Primary	56.7	53.7	14.5	14.8	39.4	5.8
Middle	36.0	28.2	8.7	17.8	83.4	32.5

Source: Government of Pakistan (2003a, pp. 3-5).
Notes: Non-government schools are mostly mixed rather than separate gender schools and hence there is no disaggregation by gender reported.

By 2000–2001, non-government enrollments were 57 per cent and 54 per cent of the total respectively for boys and girls at the primary level in urban areas. Rural primary schooling was still the domain of the public sector with the non-government sector still accounting for only about 15 per cent of total enrollments. Public sector enrollments still exceeded those of the non-government sector at the middle level across the board though again by much more in the rural areas. However, non-government sector institutions were 83.4 per cent of the total at the middle level in the urban areas and this accounted for their low student-teacher and student-institution ratios. Non-government sector institutions appear to have over-expanded at the middle level in urban areas and did not keep pace with the rapid pace of enrollments at the primary level in urban areas.

Summary and conclusions

One of the major fears of the World Bank and IMF led structural adjustment is that austerity drives imposed to attain a fiscal balance result in massive cuts in the social sectors. The expenditure as a percentage of GDP and the expenditure-to-allocation ratio show this to be the case during the Ninth Plan Period (1998–2003).

Responding to critiques, the World Bank attempted to put a human face on the economic reforms it propagates and a central element in this endeavor is protecting social sector expenditures. In Pakistan, the World Bank-led attempt at putting a human face to economic reforms took the form of the Social Action Program (SAP) which the

Government of Pakistan fully supported and for which it provided about four-fifths of the total funding in phase II. SAP's major goals were to protect social sector expenditures and to ensure that such expenditures resulted in the closing of the income, gender, and regional gaps in access to social sector facilities. The first phase of SAP ran from 1993–1996 and the second phase from 1996–2000. The program was discontinued in 2000 following a donor review, allegedly due to misappropriation of funds.

The evidence from the education sector shows that there were some successes in the education sector during the SAP period, but that there were dramatic failures. Education expenditure as a percentage of GDP rose by 0.2 per cent between the benchmark year (1993-94) and last year (1996-97) of the first phase of SAP. However, by 1998-99 it had once again declined to the pre-SAP level (2.2 per cent of GNP) despite SAP protection and continued to decline and reached 1.7 per cent by 2002–2003.

Aggregate analysis suggests that these expenditures have not been adequate to reduce congestion for both boys and girls at the middle level. By 1996-97, 83 per cent of boys and 60 per cent of girls in the 10-14 age group attended school at some point. Also, since such attendance was much higher among the younger than the older cohorts, the situation improved over time. Thus while overall school attendance for the 10-14 cohort was 72 per cent, it was 20 per cent in the 60 plus cohort. Also, evidence suggests that dropping-out is no longer as severe a problem as it used to be. Thus non-completion at the primary level was 13 per cent for males and 8 per cent for females in 1996-97. Evidence also shows that the gender and regional gap in schooling closed over the SAP period. In addition to this, evidence shows that, over the last three years of SAPP-I (1993–1996), there were improvements in various school characteristics including increases in staff and classrooms and improvement in the maintenance of the buildings and availability of books. Finally, there was a notable increase in gross enrollment rates of rural girls including those belonging to the lowest income group.

Even so, there was still much to worry about. The net rural primary enrollment rate declined during the SAP years from 50 per cent to 43 per cent for boys and 31 per cent to 30 per cent for girls. This failing is actually more profound than it appears since it does not take into account the performance of non-government schools. Non-government enrollments grew by 61 per cent and 131 per cent for girls and boys compared to 23 per cent and 4 per cent respectively for government school. Also, government schools lagged behind non-government schools in various respects. For example, only 55 per cent of rural government primary teaching occurred in a classroom compared to 82 per cent for non-government schools; 17 per cent of government schools provided desks to students compared to 70 per cent of non-government schools; 17 per cent of government schools had water supply compared to 71 per cent for non-government schools; 27 per cent of government schools had electricity compared to 88 per cent for non-government schools.

The most serious failing of SAP was its inability to address the problem of exclusion from schooling resulting from the low income of parents. In all provinces, gross and net enrollment rates were notably higher among the higher income group households. School being too expensive, or children needed to help at home or at work, were the most frequently cited subjective responses explaining why children were not in school. Again, the likelihood of dropping-out increased as the income of the household declined. Finally, the income gap in enrollments for both rural and urban girls dramatically increased over the SAP period. Thus, in this regard, SAP failed in one of the main stated goals of addressing the income gap in social sector provision. Among other approaches, fee waivers, free uniforms or a no-uniform policy, free books and supplies for the poorest, implemented by parent-run school management committees, may be the most effective and least susceptible to subversion and leakage.

References

Amalric, F., 1998, 'The Sustainable Livelihoods Approach: General Approach of the Sustainable Livelihoods Project, 1995–1997', mimeo, Society for International Development, Rome.

Banuri, T., S. R. Khan and M. Mahmood, 1997, *Just Development: Beyond Adjustment with a Human Face* (Karachi: Oxford University Press).

Carnoy, M., 1995, 'Structural Adjustment and the Changing Face of Education', *International Labor Review*, Vol. 134, No. 6, pp. 653-73.

Cornia, G. A., R. Jolly and F. Stewart, 1987, *Adjustment with a Human Face: Protecting the Vulnerable and Promoting Growth* (Oxford: Clarendon Press).

Government of Pakistan, 1994, *Economic Survey 1992-93*, Federal Bureau of Statistics, Islamabad.

Government of Pakistan, 2004, *Economic Survey 2003–2004*, Federal Bureau of Statistics, Islamabad.

Government of Pakistan, 1998, 'Education Sector Performance in the 1990s: Analysis from the PIHS', Federal Bureau of Statistics, Islamabad.

Government of Pakistan, n.d., 'Pakistan Household Integrated Survey, Round 2: 1996-97', Federal Bureau of Statistics, Islamabad.

Government of Pakistan, 2002, 'Pakistan Household Integrated Survey', Federal Bureau of Statistics, Islamabad.

Government of Pakistan, 1997, 'Report on Social Action Programme for Pakistan Consortium 1997-98', Planning Commission, Islamabad.

Government of Pakistan, 2003a, 'School Education Statistics 2000–2001, National Educational Planning and Management', Academy of Educational Planning and Management, Ministry of Education, Islamabad.

Haq, M and K. Haq, 1998, *Human Development in South Asia* (Karachi: Oxford University Press).

Khan, S. R., R. Siddiqui and F. Hussain, 1987, 'An Analysis of School Level Drop-Out Rates and Output in Pakistan,' *Pakistan Economic and Social Review*, Vol. XXV, No. 1, pp. 1-20.

Khan, S. R, 1999 'An Assessment of Basic Education under the Social Action Plan in Pakistan', *The Lahore Journal of Economics*, Vol. 4, No. 2.

Kremer, M., 2003, 'Randomized Evaluations of Educational Programs in Developing Countries: Some Lessons', *The American Economic Review*, Vol. 92, No. 2., pp. 102-106.

Social Policy and Development Center, 1998, *Social Development in Pakistan: Annual Review 1998* (Karachi: SPDC).

Sustainable Development Policy Institute, 1995, *Nature, Power, People: Citizen's Report on Sustainable Development* (Islamabad: SDPI).

UNDP, 1999, *Human Development Report 1999* (Oxford: Oxford University Press).

UNDP, 2003, *Human Development Report 2003* (Oxford: Oxford University Press).

Van de Walle, D. and K. Nead, Eds., 1995, *Public Spending and the Poor* (Baltimore: John Hopkins University Press).

World Bank, 1998, 'Implementation Completion Report: Social Action Program Project', Poverty Reduction and Economic Management Division, South Asia, Washington DC.

World Bank, 1998a, 'Project Appraisal Document: Second Social Action Program Project', Education Sector Unit, South Asia Region, Report No. 17398-PAK, Washington DC.

World Bank, 1994, 'Staff Appraisal Report: Social Action Program Project', Population and Human Resources Division, South Asia Region, Report No. 12588-PAK, Washington DC.

World Bank, 1997, 'Towards a Strategy for Elementary Education', Population and Human Resource Development Division, South Asia Region, Washington DC.

NOTES

1. This chapter is based on an updated version of Khan (1999).
2. For an official statement see Government of Pakistan, (1994, pp. 137-44 and 1998, pp. 16-17). For the Bank perspective see World Bank (1998).
3. SAP was the overall government initiated Social Action Program while SAPP-I and SAPP-II were the first and second partially donor funded Social Action Program Projects in the SAP framework.
4. Government of Pakistan, (1997).
5. Non-government schools include commercial and non-profit (NGO) schools. For definitions, refer to the Introduction.
6. World Bank (1994, p. 2).
7. The scarcity of jobs give rise to social institutions such as patronage-jobs, which in turn have a negative impact on incentives to acquire education.
8. Amalric (1998). There is acknowledgement of this in the more recent Bank literature like The World Development Report 2003.
9. Carnoy (1995, p. 662) and World Bank (1997, p. 18).
10. We concentrate on broad impact indicators since that is of essence. SAP instituted an elaborate monitoring and evaluation system and also third-party validation (by the Auditor-General's office) of input, process, output and impact. For details, see World Bank (1998, pp. 6-8).
11. Haq and Haq (1998, p. 51) suggest that 50 per cent of children dropout before completing the primary level and SPDC (1998, p. 50) similarly suggests the presence of a very high dropout rate. This impression could be based on earlier research. Khan, Siddiqui and Husain (1987, p. 9) showed very high cumulative dropout rates for 1978-79/1982-83 using provincial class level data and the cohort method to compute dropout rates. For example, for rural girls and boys at the primary level, these ranged from 54 per cent to 80 per cent and 42 per cent to 75 per cent respectively across the four provinces.
12. The indirect expense is what parents forego in potential help with chores or earnings from work when the child is in school.
13. The reader is reminded that gross enrollment rate is defined as the number of children attending the primary level (i.e. class 0-5) divided by the number of children in the 5-10 cohort, converted into a percentage. Net enrollment rate is defined as the number of children in the 5-10 age cohort attending the primary level divided by the number of children in the 5-10 age cohort converted into a percentage. Thus, the increases in net enrollment rates provide a more precise indicator of educational success. Note that it is possible for total absolute enrollments and gross enrollment rates to rise while net enrollment rates are declining.
14. Government of Pakistan (1998, p. 42) established a positive and significant association of income and school attendance for boys and girls in both urban and rural areas using multivariate analysis.
15. Government of Pakistan (n.d., p. 33). Quintiles were derived based on per capita household consumption and the derivation is included in Appendix C of the cited report.
16. While 6 and 25 per cent respectively of children in urban and rural areas from the highest quintile dropped out before completing class 6, these percentages were 24

per cent and 50 per cent respectively for the lowest quintile [FBS, PIHS (1998, p. 41)].

17. Salman Zaidi did the data analysis for 1991 and 1995-96.

18. Other less prominent reasons in explaining non-attendance and non-completion for girls were parental disapproval and distance from school. Among the important outliers was the mention of 'education not being useful' for girls in rural Balochistan and for boys in rural Punjab.

19. Follow-up research in Pakistan for investigating the impact of these incentives on educational attainment would be useful. Refer to Kremer (2003) for an evaluation of such programs.

20. For a comprehensive study of targeting, see eds. Van de Walle and Nead (1995). One lesson that emerges from this volume is that targeting is complex. In the opening piece of this volume, Sen (pp. 11-25) identifies several problems of targeting including corruption, stigma, exclusion, dependency, counteracting behavioral changes, administrative cost, and lack of political support. With regard to the targeting, we propose waiving all fees is more straightforward than providing uniforms, books, and supplies.

21. Refer to chapter 3 for more details on community participation via SMCs in Pakistan.

22. These aggregate numbers do not indicate the real 'dualism' of educational quality and the resultant social and economic opportunities in elite urban schools and cash-strapped government schools. For an account of educational dualism, refer to SDPI (1995, pp. 211-13).

2 [1]

A Qualitative Analysis of Government, NGO and Private Rural Primary Schools

2.1. Introduction

It is often stated that NGOs are more effective in the delivery of services than the government and, indeed, our field observations show that, in many respects, this was the case in the delivery of basic education. However, while there are many assertions about the performance of NGOs based on a handful of case studies, anecdotes and preconceived notions, to date there is little systematic sector-specific information comparing the performance of NGOs with the government and private sectors.[2]

Not much is known either about rural private sector schooling.[3] Anecdotal evidence suggests that this is a rapidly growing sector. Some assert that such schools cheat gullible rural folk with a smattering of English on the syllabus and the status symbols represented by private sector uniforms. Others extol the dedication of private sector teachers. Either way, it is necessary to more systematically assess the contribution of such schools, their potential for growth, the lessons derived from their practice and the social implications of their presence.

In section 2, we describe the conceptual framework, in section 3, we provide a quantitative overview of NGO and private schools based on our survey data. In section 4, the qualitative results, primarily based on field evaluations, are presented. In section 5, we propose reform options based on our findings. We end with a summary and some concluding remarks. Six case studies of the 129 used for the qualitative section, representing the best and worst of each type of school, are presented in Annex 2.2 to illustrate the nature of the qualitative data set used for this chapter.

2.2. Conceptual framework

The conceptual framework we used for viewing the vast and rich observations that emerged from the field reports is the 'principal-agent model'.[4] In the 'principal-agent' context, the principal relies on the agent to execute the principal's agenda. A good outcome is likely when the agent has appropriate incentives to carry out the agenda of the principal rather then carrying out an independent agenda. Thus the 'principal-agent' problem can be viewed as one of ensuring that there is agenda compatibility.

The 'principal-agent' problem occurs in the theory of the firm when the interests of the stock owners and the interests of the hired managers do not coincide. The challenge is to structure incentives in a way so that the two interests are merged. Providing part of the remuneration in the form of stock options could be a solution to the problem of incentives of owners and managers diverging.[5] Again, even if the owners and managers have unified objectives, the interests of the managers and those of the workers may deviate. One solution to the latter problem is to make the returns to workers tied to the profit of the firm. In this way, in theory, a harmony of interests may be achieved across the board by linking all remuneration to profits.

In government schooling, the principal is the public that, via a circular process, has to ensure good government service. In a practical sense, the public mandate is entrusted to the ministry of education as the line agency of the provincial governments. Authority for management and enforcement devolves down the hierarchy to the district and assistant education officers (DEO/AEO) and the field supervisors who are entrusted with the task of monitoring and enforcement. One could view the school administration, heads and teachers as agents for providing good schooling. The public's mechanisms for enforcement are complaints (voice), social sanctions if there is some community influence on teachers and government officials, withdrawal if there is an alternative to government schooling (exit),[6] or ultimately not voting for an inefficient government.

As explained in chapter 1, voice and social sanction options have seriously weakened in Pakistan as rich parents have abandoned government schools in favor of private or NGO schools.[7] The remaining students are generally from the lower income households and therefore the exit option is not an option for them either.[8] Finally, the electoral option is a weak and crude enforcement mechanism for several reasons.

First, concerned ministry officials may remain completely unaffected by a change in government, particularly at the lower administrative level. Second, even if poor performance was signaled by the public, tenure- and seniority-based pay protects civil service employees, including teachers who do not perform well (see chapter 5). Third, in practice, elections are an unlikely tool for such signaling. Voting behavior is complex and determined by many influences and, even if failure in social sector delivery plays a part in it, the message is likely to get lost. Devolved power to the grassroots level could be a viable control mechanism based on public oversight.[9]

In a 'principal-agent' framework, success would mean that the provincial and local governments internalize what the public interest is and deliver on it. Given the diffuse signals and weak enforcement mechanism referred to above, public-spiritedness needs to be internalized by senior civil service officials independently such that they become the 'principals'. While it is easy to monitor teacher attendance, it is very difficult to contract for the more meaningful aspects of the job, such as empathy for the children. In this situation, much depends on effective hiring criteria for teachers.

In private schools, the 'principal' is the owner with reference to profit maximization. The 'principal' is often also the school administrator or school head. As long as there is competition, there is an identity of interests between owners and parents since good schooling is what parents want and that is also what will produce demand and high profits for the owners. Parents seeking alternative schooling for their children is the enforcement mechanism for good schooling. In the absence of competition, complaints (voice) are all parents can resort to and there is no guarantee that this will meet with a response.

Assuming that there is competition, and therefore a convergence of parent and owner interests, good schooling depends on, among other things, how effectively the 'principal' motivates the 'agents' (teachers). Sound selection, good training, and appropriate remuneration are among the tools that can be used for motivating teachers. However, threat of termination is an alternative tool for motivating teachers, and this is the one that we found was used more frequently.

The 'principals' in one school NGOs may operate much like private sector schools. A mission rather than profit may drive the individuals and this could be another source of motivation for the teachers as 'agents' if they identify with the mission. In multi-school NGOs, the 'principal' and guardian of the mission and quality is the NGO, i.e. it assumes the public interest. It is the larger organization rather than the school that plays the role of monitor and enforcer of standards. Teacher's working conditions, training and motivation are all tools to turn them into effective 'agents'. Sometimes, the NGOs also mobilize communities to become contributors and enforcers of standards via informal channels or, more formally, via a parent-teacher association. In this case, the NGO effectively invites the community, in which the school is situated, to be a co-principal.

2.3. Comparative analysis: results from quantitative survey data[10]

We use statistics generated by our data sets in this section to identify the differences across the three types of schools. While there are some statistics based on larger samples comparing differences between government and non-government (NGO or private) schools, they are limited in scope and do not distinguish between NGO and private schools.[11]

Annex 2.1, Tables 1-4 report on the basic distinguishing features across government, NGO, and private schools in our sample. Table 1 focuses on family background, Table 2 on basic school facilities, Table 3 on school management issues, and Table 4 on teacher characteristics (class 5 teachers). On some issues such as whether teachers beat the children, provided extra help after school, or provided paid tuition after school, student responses are documented. There were 750, 608, and 693 student respondents respectively from government, private, and NGO schools. Given the large amount of information we gathered, the focus in this section is on the differences across the three schools that could account for their success or failure. After reviewing the findings of the four tables in the Annex 2.1, we juxtapose these with student performance.

Annex 2.1, Table 1 reports the socio-economic background of the parents that send their children to government, private, and NGO schools respectively. The profile of parents of children going to private and NGO schools was similar and these parents (both fathers and mothers) were better educated and wealthier than parents who send their children to government schools. For example, while 14 per cent of the children going to government schools had extremely poor parents, this was the case for only about 5 per cent of the children going to private and NGO schools respectively. Similarly, while less than 3 per cent of the children going to government schools had rich parents; this was the case for 17 and 15 per cent of children going to private and NGO schools respectively.

Annex 2.1, Table 2 reports on basic facilities like desks, chairs, facilities for teachers, accommodation, fans, electricity, drinking water, washrooms, charts, models, and libraries available in the three types of schools. Across the board, NGO schools had the best facilities followed by private schools.

Annex 2.1, Table 3 explores management and policy issues. As expected, private and NGO schools were much more likely to innovate with the curriculum and less likely to use the mother tongue, as opposed to the national language, as a medium of instruction. There was also a much greater likelihood that parents checked the homework and saw the report card in private and NGO schools. Multi-grade teaching is an economy measure but also viewed as a hindrance to learning. This practice was much more widespread in private schools (42 per cent) than in government (27 per cent) or NGO schools (20 per cent). The percentage of children who were subjected to corporal punishment in NGO schools was the lowest at 37 per cent (though still high) compared to 48 per cent and 46 per cent respectively for government and private schools.

The average monthly tuition fees, as expected, were much lower in government schools (Rs 29) compared to private schools (Rs 121). The surprise was that NGO average monthly fee (Rs 108) was almost as high as that of the private schools. The unexpectedly high fee results from the expressed requirement of donors to have their interventions attain financial sustainability as soon as possible. However, the percentage of poor students paying fees in NGO schools at 23 per cent was much lower than private schools (44 per cent), and the fee charged from poor parents was nominal.

Teachers are most important to education at any level and Annex 2.1, Table 4 reports on key teacher characteristics. Mean teacher salaries in government schools were almost twice as high as private schools and almost a third as much more than NGO schools. Also, average teacher experience in government schools was almost twice that in NGO schools. Teacher qualifications were roughly similar in NGO and government schools, both somewhat higher than private school teachers in terms of teachers possessing a bachelors or masters degree. In-service training was the highest for NGO teachers while pre-service training was highest for government schools teachers. Thus, it is evident that private schools paid their teachers the least and invested the least in them.

The mean absentee rates for teachers at 11.67 days per year were the highest in government schools compared to 10.74 and 5.86 for private schools and NGO schools respectively. Thus, the mean teacher absentee rates in government and private schools were almost double those in NGO schools and this may be a result of the higher level of motivation among NGO teachers. The mean student absentee rates were 6.1, 10.1 and 5.4 days respectively for government, private, and NGO schools and so once again the lowest for NGO schools. The mean student dropout rate since the beginning of the class year in class 5 was again lowest for NGO schools at less than one student compared to 1.5 and 3 for government and private schools. In addition, as reported above, NGO schools had the best facilities and invested the most in the training of their teachers once hired. The question that follows naturally is whether any of this showed up in a better performance of students in NGO schools. The results of the tests administered by the field teams are reported below in Table 2.1.

Table 2.1 Percentage marks on comprehension and math tests for teachers and class 3 and class 5 students by school type.

Type of School	Teacher scores		Students scores, Class 3		Student scores, Class 5	
	Math	Comp.	Math	Comp.	Math	Comp.
NGO	5.9	24.5	2.6	10.1	4.9	16.7
	(2.7)	(3.3)	(1.2)	(4.9)	(1.3)	(3.6)
Private	6.1	23.1	2.4	7.1	4.5	13.6
	(3.0)	(5.3)	(1.2)	(3.7)	(1.7)	(4.4)
Govt.	5.3	23.2	1.5	4.2	3.8	10.1
	(3.0)	(4.7)	(1.3)	(3.4)	(1.8)	(4.7)

Source: SDPI Survey, 1998.
Notes: Comprehension and math tests for students were developed using the syllabi of class 3 and class 5 of various textbook boards. Comprehension test for teachers was taken from an IFPRI project on education in rural Pakistan [Alderman et al., (1995)], whereas a math test from the same project was adapted based on pre-tests.
   Figures in parentheses are standard deviations on mean scores for teachers and mean of class mean scores for students across schools. The maximum scores on teacher tests were 10 and 30, and on student tests 10 and 25 for math and comprehension respectively.

In terms of overall performance, the low math scores across the board are shocking as is the low comprehension score for class 3 in government schools. In a comparative context, several points are evident from Table 2.1. First, children in NGO schools had the best mean performance in both subjects and both classes. Second, on average, government school students had a much lower scale of academic achievement in class 3 and this remained true on an absolute level by class 5. However, the relative gain in scores between class 3 and class 5 was much higher in government schools and that is suggestive of the potential for improvement. Third, the variation in scores among students for government schools was generally the highest or close to the highest and it was the lowest or close to the lowest for NGO schools. Finally, as a qualifier, it is interesting that the incidence of cheating among students and teachers was highest in government schools and lowest in NGO schools and so government teacher and student scores are exaggerated.[12] In the sections that follow, we review the qualitative findings regarding three different kinds of schools, which is the main focus of this chapter.

2.4. Comparative analysis: results from qualitative survey data

We start out with a summary evaluation by the field team. The criterion they used for assessing success included the performance of class 3 and class 5 students and class 5 teachers on comprehension and math tests reported above in Table 2.1, the state of discipline and confidence of students, motivation, dedication, training and experience of teachers, whether students and/or teachers cheated in the tests, physical facilities of the school, availability of school supplies and the quality of school administration and management. This evaluation, presented below in Table 2.2, is a general impression based on the above criterion and not based on developing indices that would be subjective anyway.

Table 2.2 A comparison of the success and failure of government, private, and NGO schools

Type of school	Evaluation		
	Successful	Not successful	In-between
Government	5	32	6
Private	19	17	7
NGO	31	8	4

Source: Survey field-team evaluation, 1998.

The table above indicates that NGO schools were the most likely to be successful followed by private schools. That only five out of forty-three government schools were viewed as successful confirms what is now well known, i.e. that the state of government sector basic education is abysmal and urgently in need of reform. We turn now to an evaluation of field reports by school type.

2.4.1. Government schools

The poor showing of government schools is a serious cause for concern if we view 'evening the odds' as a fundamental state responsibility. The clients of government schools are generally poor and illiterate.[13] As earlier indicated, the richer parents are abandoning government schools in droves. This is consistent with the better-off parents indicating to us that government schools were incapable of providing a decent education. The poor parents were often aware of the bad standard of education being offered to their wards, but were unable to do much about this because of their economic circumstances. Even then, we noticed that many relatively poor parents stretched their resources to provide a non-government education to their children either out of genuine concern for their children's education, or sometimes, because non-government education has become a mark of status in rural society. Often, it was the bright children that parents removed from government schools.

This exodus of the richer children and the brighter, poor children to non-government schools is accentuating the crisis of government sector education. The wealthier parents are the most likely to complain and play a 'principal's' role in maintaining standards. The brighter children are the most likely to raise the general level of the class. With these sources of countervailing pressure gone, rural government sector education will deteriorate further. Thus, the children of poor parents often do not make it to school and, those that do, have little hope of getting very far in an increasingly competitive world.[14]

Concerned and interested parents of children in government schools were generally the exception rather than the rule. Thus teachers got away with educational murder. Not only did they wantonly neglect their duties, they also used students to do their chores and bring gratuities. They also charged special illegal fees and ran their own businesses on the side. Focus group meetings often showed illiterate and poor parents satisfied because they did not know any better. Often they seemed content that their children were in school and at other times they seemed to view the school as a convenient child-sitting arrangement. However, even this service was not reliable, since many parents and communities complained that students came and went as they pleased and this was confirmed by field observation.

While government teachers were more highly paid than non-government teachers, some parents were under the impression that government teachers were very poorly paid and hence had no option but to run independent businesses on the side to supplement their meager income.[15] However, being paid more than private sector teachers does not constitute good pay.[16]

One issue that parents and the community dwelt on was whether or not the teachers were from the village. Teachers who did not reside in the village were often late and absent. However, they were less likely to be harsh to children of a particular *biradari* (clan) and more receptive to complaints from the parents about the schooling. Thus overall, they were viewed as more effective.

The surprise visitor to a government school is likely to confront very poor facilities, very high student and teacher absenteeism, gossiping and disinterested teachers and an unrestrained student body running wild.[17] Teachers and parents blamed each other for a lack of interest. There are elements of truth to both allegations. However, reform needs to start in the school and filter out to the home. An angry and accusing household or a disinterested household is not likely to be a very receptive one.

The power of teachers, among other factors, undermines government sector schooling. There are at least five sources of teacher power. First, the teachers as government servants have tenure and thus face little threat of losing their jobs if they perform poorly. Second, there is very little supervision by education officers so teachers feel secure in their neglect. Third, even if they are caught out, they find political authorities to protect them. Fourth, even if they don't have political connections, they have a teacher's association running interference for them. Fifth, they face a very poor and uneducated constituency of parents, which provides no threat or countervailing power. Thus, under current circumstances, government sector teachers are unlikely to be good 'agents'.

2.4.2. Private schools

Private schools presented the greatest contrast in performance. The worst ones were often run as a family business with rented buildings that were completely inadequate for schooling. These buildings were crowded, poorly ventilated, poorly lit, hot, short of even poor quality furniture, had dirty bathrooms, no clean drinking water and no play area.[18] By contrast, some schools even had well-stocked libraries that they encouraged students to use, and computers for instructing the higher grades.

The teachers were often paid poorly, not trained and made to work hard.[19] Several teachers complained about their poor pay and the turnover rate was stated to be high. The higher paid, much more relaxed and tenured government teaching positions were obviously very attractive. A year or two of teaching in private schools was viewed as enough to establish credentials for a more secure government job.

Yet despite this, teachers were very often industrious, disciplined and motivated. The threat of job loss no doubt had something to do with this. Students were also generally disciplined, confident and well turned-out, even if the performance on the tests was not good. Homework was in general regularly assigned and corrected, something the parents noted and greatly appreciated. Parent-teacher contact was much higher and the school administration much more responsive to parental concerns but this was not institutionalized.[20] However, teachers in general made more effort to apprise parents of the child's performance. High absenteeism was the exception rather than the rule.

While fees were in general much higher than in government schools and too high for the poor, several schools ran scholarship programs for the able, poor students and had concession-based fee structures.[21] The curse of private tuition after school was rife with many of the richer parents, perhaps as a substitute to giving their own time, and many teachers supplemented their income with it.

Private schools were often able to get away with poor performance because relatively uneducated parents had only abysmal government sector schooling to compare private schooling with. Indeed, much of the discussion of focus group meetings with parents whose children were in NGO and private schools centered on the disastrous state of government sector schooling. Many put their children in a private school as much from a vague sense of doing the best by their child as for the status symbol this has come to represent. Parents took great pride in books on the syllabus that had been published by a multi-national publisher. More disturbing, poor parents sometimes judged quality by the fee they were paying. In some community focus group meetings, parents suggested that government schooling should be abolished and subsidies provided to non-government schools to make them more affordable.[22]

The better educated parents were often more vocal, expected higher standards and complained bitterly since they were paying what they perceived to be a high price. In some cases, even illiterate parents who were paying what they viewed as very high fees had high expectations and were vocal about what they perceived as an inadequate service.[23] School Management Committees (SMCs) were largely irrelevant for private schools (Annex 2.1, Table 3). Parents felt they were paying a good price and that is where their responsibility ended. In turn, they expected the school to deliver the education. This was true across the board in a majority of schools surveyed, but not surprisingly, was more the case with private sector schools.

The field team found cheating by students and even teachers (taking help from colleagues) much more prevalent in government and private schools. Private school teachers operating in a 'for profit' environment probably felt under pressure to be able to show good results. Thus bribing authorities to show good results or grade inflation were among the practices observed.

The essential point in good performance was good management and, more often than not, this hinged on an exceptional and dedicated 'principal' or administrator who exercised supervision and led by example. Such individuals were often concerned with infusing a high moral character in children; something the community focus groups were highly appreciative of. Staff that taught in schools that they had themselves attended, whether in the private or government sectors, often developed an emotional attachment and worked hard.

2.4.3. NGO schools[24]

NGO schooling was in many respects the most successful (see Table 2.1 for performance). However, not all NGO schools visited were a success. We classified NGO schools in our sample based on whether they were single-school NGOs or part of a multi-school program with a support system. The latter often resulted in better management. Within these categories, we found schools that had a secular, religious or ideological orientation. The ideological orientation was important in understanding NGO motivation and this distinguished the prominent multi-school NGO programs from the for-profit private schools in most cases.

NGO schools were viewed as private schools in the public perception and educating a child in an NGO school also represented a 'status symbol'. While NGO fees were comparable to that of private schools (Rs 108 compared to Rs 121 for private schools) 77 per cent of NGO schools did not require poor students to pay a fee, and others charged a nominal fee, compared to 56 per cent of private schools that followed such a practice (Annex 2.1, Table 3). There is thus a real distinction in fees between schools run for profit compared to those operating on a non-profit basis.

The unsuccessful single-school NGOs

These schools had practices similar to the unsuccessful private schools. The schools were often in rented buildings that were crowded and totally inappropriate for schooling. The notorious teacher practice of ignoring students in class and then giving after-school tuition for a fee was witnessed in such NGO schools as in private schools.

The successful single-school NGOs

There were several examples of successful single-school NGOs where practices differed from those mentioned in the sub-section above. School established by an association of teachers only hired teachers that had earned an intermediate degree (A-level equivalent) as a minimum qualification and had been trained as teachers. Discipline was good and the students were well-behaved and enthusiastic. The student-teacher rapport was notable and this was probably facilitated by the joint projects that they engaged in. The Green Foundation School stood out because of its highly equipped large building, impressive library and very qualified teachers. In both schools, the poor parents felt burdened by the fees, and the very poor regretted being excluded.

An NGO ran a successful school in Tharparker catering mainly to a Hindu community. They had to work very hard to convince the community to allow females to teach in the school. However, they were successful and managed to get together a team of qualified, well-trained, and committed teachers. The proud parents felt that, as a result, their offspring were getting an education that would make them capable of even competing with students from Karachi, Pakistan's biggest city.

The Bluebird Grammar School in Swabi was impressive. The school building and classes were good, and students were in clean uniforms and well-disciplined. All students on the register were present on the day of the field visit. Another surprise for the field team was that the toilets even had soap and towels. Most of the teachers had earned a masters' degree and were dedicated and competent. The team spirit observed among teachers was commendable and student-teacher relations were friendly. The school provided free education to responsive students and had plans to start computer classes. The parents' participated in school activities and the school administration was responsive to parent's suggestions. The parents were very satisfied and mentioned that their children seemed dull before they started attending this school. Due to the higher standard, the school often made children transferring in from government schools stay back in the same class.

The Northern Public School in Swabi was partially funded by a women's welfare organization and hence, compared to the private sector schools, charged more modest fees. While the rented apartment building was not completely adequate and the teachers were not trained, both students and teachers did very well in the tests. The teachers also tried to inculcate good habits like manners, punctuality, and cleanliness. Witnessing a student carry a piece of torn paper to the dustbin was a surprise for one field-team member. The parents attributed success to the supervision of the principal.

The badly managed multi-school NGO programs

One Anjuman (association) had adopted thirteen primary schools at the time of the field visit, but most were new and only one of these had students in class 5. The student-teacher rapport seemed good, but the community was quite negative about the casual attitude of the school administration. No one seemed aware of the role of the Anjuman in managing the school. One community member thought that the school was just a tax break for the owner of the nearby fruit farm. Parents thought the fee was too high for the product delivered, and some mentioned they would transfer their child, perhaps even to a government school.

Five out of the six schools, founded by a private association of teachers, in our sample were successful. The sixth was like the typical, unsuccessful private sector school. The classrooms were narrow and dark, and multi-grade teaching was being practiced. Students lacked discipline and the teachers seemed disinterested. Parents were not literate and seemed unable to discern what represented educational quality. The religious affiliation of the school was, however, a source of comfort for parents, and they willingly sent their daughters to the school.

Two of the four schools run by an old and well-established NGO in Sindh province were no different from the shoddy private sector schools. In one of the two schools, teacher training was poor and students were found giving tuition after school. While there was a general body (twenty-six NGO and community members) to run the school, it made little difference to the school's functioning. In the other school, management by the NGO was very lax. No attendance register was maintained and teachers routinely came late. Four of the classes were being held in a veranda, which made concentration difficult for teachers and students. Class 3 students were unable to read the math and comprehension tests in Sindhi, even though that was the medium of instruction. While 10 per cent of the students were supposed to be allowed to attend free, students had dropped out because they could not afford the fee. The community had been mobilized and was fully involved, interested and active and represented on the PTA. They had given the land and contributed towards the cost of the building and, despite the poor performance of the school, were willing to continue contributing.

The well-managed multi-school religious NGO programs

There were two Educational & Welfare Society schools in the sample and the NGO management was sound. The teachers were very professional and committed even though not highly qualified. The principal was also very dedicated and professional and conducted teacher training. The fee structure was perceived by the community to be reasonable. They also appreciated the well-equipped computer lab. The Sunni households noted the sectarian (Shia) orientation of the schools (parents were asked to sign release forms), but they were content with the education and satisfied with countering the sectarian influence via religious education at home. The NGO exercised good supervision, although excess demand had started resulting in over-crowding. Nonetheless, the parents noted the tremendous progress made by their children since they had been shifted to this school.

The five successful schools run by the association of teachers were individualized. There seemed to be no overarching organizational presence of the parent NGO performing the supervisory role. The teachers in some schools were not highly qualified but were dedicated and managed to infuse confidence in the students who were well dressed and well behaved. By contrast to the crowded rented buildings and poorly qualified teachers of some schools, others had spacious and well-equipped classes and highly qualified and hard-working teachers.

Poor parents felt pinched by the fees that the school administration said was necessary to cover recurrent expenditures. In one school, poor students were allowed to attend free and the community contributed for scholarships for very poor, deserving students. In another, an elaborate fee structure was adopted to accommodate the poor students. Some parents nonetheless complained about the high fees. Two of the three partners running one school, originally started as a 'for-profit' school, showed concern that the school was not recovering costs. The parents across the board were very supportive of the religious orientation of the schools. In this regard, the schools could get away with poor delivery as indicated by one school described in the last sub-section.

Modern Schools is probably one of the best examples of a multi-school program that consistently produced good results. The parents supported the religious orientation and education, and the efforts of the school to inculcate a moral outlook among the students. Modern Schools were well managed with the NGO playing the role of a monitor and enforcer of standards. The schools buildings were purpose-built and hence had all the facilities necessary for good schooling. Compared to government schools, this meant that they were well lit, properly ventilated, had appropriate furniture for the students and teachers, and the classes were of a comfortable size and not crowded. One comment about the students was that they were disciplined, self-confident, and had a spark rare in rural schools. The teachers were motivated, aware, involved, knew the parents, and put in a great deal of effort.

A systematic policy to curb absenteeism was observed. The students were admonished twice and, if this did not work, a letter was written to the parents to discuss the issue. Expulsion was maintained as the last option. There was regular testing of students to keep them involved and alert. Extra periods were observed after school to provide special assistance to weak students.

In some cases, a strong and involved SMC, composed of village notables, addressed parental concerns. These were educated individuals who gave adequate time to the school. Interestingly, the NGO did not encourage collective action by the community and, in one case, discouraged a fund raising effort by the community for a school building. It may be that this effort competed with what the NGO was there to provide.

Other well-managed multi-school NGO programs

The Whitefield Public School was one of a chain of over fifteen schools run by a public welfare society in Balochistan. It battled odds to deliver a good education. A hall in a rented building was divided into classes, and so the noise level was very high. Nonetheless, the teachers were well paid, worked hard, and performed well. The parents appreciated the good education. Although they found the fees high, the government school alternative was not considered acceptable. They appreciated and participated actively in the functions organized by the school. The administration was responsive to the parents and welcomed their inputs for improvements.

Two Bright Star schools in Sindh were successful. They showed better performance among class 3 relative to class 5 students because the latter attained their earlier schooling elsewhere. These schools took pains with teacher training which was given for two weeks twice a year.

In the two successful schools, the community pointed to the dedication of the teachers as making a difference in both cases. In one school, the principal had spent her life in the education department and retired after a stint as a DEO (district education officer). She had instituted a policy of turning back students arriving late. Parents resented the wastage of the fare but appreciated the discipline among the teachers and students. The other school was successful despite the description of the school by the field team as 'small, cramped, dingy, damp, dirty, and rat infested'.

The importance of the exceptional individual shines through when assessing success. This could be a dedicated principal or motivated administrator. However, even more important was good overall management. Schools run by two private organizations were outstanding in conditions where government and private schooling were disasters. The facilities and teacher training provided and the monitoring systems established delivered good schooling with great consistency.

One of these targeted the most deprived peri-urban and rural communities and hence the schools were built in very poor neighborhoods. One description of an imposing structure was that it was a 'palace amidst huts' in an area that was 'humming with flies and had people playing cards and board-games on the streets'. The purpose-built schools, costing up to Rs 2.5 million, were fully equipped including art rooms for the junior section. The rooms were large and airy, had good furniture, and all necessary charts and aids, including audio aids, were available and in use.

Free milk and cookies were provided several times a week; the frequency determined by how poor the community was. In one neighborhood, parents could not afford to feed the children before sending them to school. The fees were tailored to the income of the parents such that 5 per cent of household income was charged. The school maintained all the relevant data concerning the students and the parents. Uniforms were provided free and books provided on credit on very easy terms.

Both the teachers and students were in uniform. The teachers were confident and treated well including being given a 'pick-up and drop' service. However, in return, they were expected to work hard and prepare monthly and annual work-plans. Teachers attended monthly meetings to present performance reports and problems were discussed with the NGO education specialist. They were given three months of intensive teacher training and bi-annual refresher courses.

There was no formal PTA but a parent association (PA) was formed to contain high dropout rates and to encourage enrollments. The school administration was very responsive to the parents and kept them posted on the child's progress, but the PA had no formal role in school affairs. A limit on the student-teacher ratio was strictly observed and excess demand resulted in plans for building a new school. This excess demand, which arose once the school was established, was particularly commendable given that these schools were normally built in communities where at least the fathers attached little value to schooling and would have preferred the child to help them with their own work or otherwise supplement household income.

Three schools in our sample in the Northern Areas had good facilities, science labs, well-qualified and trained teachers, and confident, hardworking, and well-behaved students. The school administration followed up the progress of the students with the parents, but also relied on very active VECs (village education committees). Thus, students absent for more than six days were referred to the VECs, which also assessed individual fees and paid the teachers' salaries. The overall monitoring and evaluation was retained by the parent organization.

These schools proved that VECs do work. The communities had been mobilized to take an interest in their children's schooling, had contributed land and labor for the school building and for on-going improvements like boundary walls, a science lab or an examination hall. They took an active on-going interest in school affairs and had the power to replace poor teachers in consultation with the NGO. In one case, a VEC blocked admission because, due to excess demand, the classes were getting overcrowded. In turn, it began consultations with the NGO to build more classrooms. It also permitted the school to use the premise for evening classes for a girl's college, since none was available for miles. Thus in all aspects, the parents performed the role of effective co-principals.

2.5. Reforming government sector basic education

Not all government schools performed poorly as indicated in Table 2.1. In Annex 2.2, Case 5, we present a case study of a very successful government school. However, the case study also explains the special circumstances of this success. We feel that with appropriate school reform, this should become the norm. Our concern is mainly with government sector schooling, which is all that the poorest now have recourse to. NGO schools seem to be doing well for the most part and, in any case; addressing problems in the NGO and private sectors pertains to the realm of regulation.

Given the very low base delivery of government schools, it was relatively easy for the NGO schools and private schools to win support from households and communities for the service they delivered. Providing effective competition and hence raising overall standards is the main reason why reforming public sector education is so essential. The impact will be felt across the board and not just in public schools, since the public sector is the base standard-bearer given its lower fees.

Based on field observations, we feel that successful reform of basic education has to tackle teacher power and parent disinterest head-on. We suggest the following:

a. Given the exodus of children from government schools and the rapid pace of expansion of non-government schooling, the public sector should now focus on quality. Thus most new resources should be allocated to upgrading and providing adequate facilities to existing government schools. Government schools uniformly seemed to have the worst facilities. Sitting on the floor in a small multi-grade class, in the veranda or under a tree can be a deterrent to learning. Even when schools did have small classrooms, the space, lighting and ventilation were very inadequate.

b. Even though public sector teacher's pay is higher than NGO and private sector schools, we suggest that the pay should be raised to attract a better quality teacher.

c. The power of the teacher association should be confined to negotiating pay and perks. *De facto* tenure should be abolished and incompetent teachers weeded out by having them sit for qualifying tests.

d. Teachers need to be assessed by enrollment rates, retention rates and the performance of their students in board exams. Principals are required to maintain such data, and it should be put to good use. We found it instructive that parent groups in all four provinces mentioned the key role of monitoring and the lack of it in government schools as being instrumental in their poor performance.

e. Since enrollment and retention rates have much to do with the household and community, the teachers will have an incentive to work with households and communities. Instead of sabotaging the PTA, they will have an incentive to use it to mobilize the community and parents. The parents in turn should have a role in ensuring that the data collected is accurate.

f. The most challenging part of schooling reform will be in ensuring the state plays its part as an effective 'co-principal'. Obviously, this issue is part of overall public sector reforms.[25] Our view is that parents can work effectively with government officials as 'co-principals' if the balance of power between government officials and parents is altered. If school officials are well paid local (rather than provincial) government officials, whose evaluation is done partly by the PTA and who are accessible to the PTA, effective monitoring and supervision becomes a possibility.

We feel that the reforms suggested above are among the minimum essential steps that are required to improve public sector schooling. However, without such steps, public sector schooling will remain a dead loss.

Summary and conclusion

Education is one of the key aspects of human development in that it qualitatively improves the nature of choices humans make over their lifetime. Thus, adult literacy has been included as one of the key indicators for quantifying human development across countries. It is now well known that education is fundamental on a national level for enhancing economic growth and reducing poverty. Individuals and households benefit from it because it enhances earnings and social mobility, improves nutrition, reduces disease, and is the door to many other benefits. Female education in particular has been shown to result in high private and social returns.

This chapter reports mainly on the qualitative results of a comparative institutional analysis of government, private, and NGO schools. One failing of the NGO sector is that they cater to families that are as well-off and more educated than the families who are the clients of private schools. Thus household characteristics could partly be the cause of the better NGO school performance. The average NGO sector school fees were comparable to that of private schools due to the pressure they confront to attain financial sustainability. However, 77 per cent of the NGOs were not charging fees from poor parents and most others charged them a nominal fee.

Our research showed that overall, the NGOs were the most successful in delivering good education. The tested performance was better, teacher and student absentee rates were lowest, in-service training the highest, teachers were the most responsive, teacher-parent interaction was the highest, the incidence of cheating was the lowest, and the school facilities were the best.

Our research also confirmed, what is now well known, that the state of government sector basic education in Pakistan is an unmitigated disaster. Further, our research shows that dealing with teacher power, good management and supervision are the keys to government sector schooling success. Teacher power is rooted in tenure, absence of supervision, political protection, poor parents with little countervailing power, and the strength of the teacher associations. Eliminating *de facto* tenure is necessary but good pay for quality teaching is also necessary. Also, the parents need to be involved as a 'co-principal' in supervision via school management committees (SMCs).

SMCs can play an important role as indicated by the schools that have worked hard to establish them. Given the general perception of parents across the board that education is the school's responsibility, one wondered if such committees could work. We found illiterate mothers hard at work at home and outside the home, and fathers returning late from work or working away from the village. Thus, it was understandable that we found such an attitude among parents. However, the hard work put in by these schools and their parent organizations in mobilizing communities turned the latter into an interested force to improve basic education and hence an effective 'co-principal'.

We found that when the multi-school NGO organization was not uniformly strong and effective, the role of a principal or key administrator could be the key to making a difference. However, when the organization was strong, the results were uniformly good and not dependent on an exceptional individual, who if present represented a bonus. Good management was also observed in some single-school NGOs, but, obviously, economies of scale were not present.

To sum up, for NGO schools, good management is the key to good performance as demonstrated by sampled multi-school NGOs. However, good management is possible for NGOs since the organization as the 'principal' is driven by a mission and exercises the supervision needed. The mission could be a dedication to the cause of education and what this represents for nation-building or the motivation to construct society in a particular image as in the case of the religious NGOs. Further, a well-known educational society has also demonstrated that community participation and collective action via a SMC and broader community interest and involvement can also be a force for good schooling.

For private schools, competition plays the role of the owner acting as the 'principal' seeking good results, since that is related to the owner's profit as long as there is competition. The government sector needs to provide the effective competition. In addition to this, the state needs to provide the necessary regulatory function and the parents need to provide the necessary 'voice' and 'social sanctions' to bring about changes and use 'exit' as a last resort option.

It would be extravagant to expect government to play the part of a 'principal' as in well-organized NGOs. However, the government may be able to deliver if parents as the concerned client can be turned into an effective 'co-principal'. The point to keep in mind is the need for genuine empowerment of parents. This will only happen if the power balance is effectively shifted away from teachers and local government officials towards parents, and if teachers and local government officials have adequate incentive to work with parents.

References

Alderman, H., J. R. Behrman, S. R. Khan, D. R. Ross and R. Sabot, 1995, 'Public Schooling Expenditures in Rural Pakistan: Efficiently Targeting Girls and a Lagging Region', in eds. D. van de Walle and K. Nead, *Public Spending and the Poor: Theory and Evidence* (Baltimore: Johns Hopkins University Press).

Andarabi, T., J. Das, and A. I. Khwaja, 2002, 'The Rise of Private Schooling in Pakistan: Catering to the Urban Elite or Educating the Rural Poor?' draft, Islamabad.

Baqir, F., 1998, 'The Role of NGOs in Education', in ed. P. Hoodbhoy, *Education and the State: Fifty Years of Pakistan* (Karachi: Oxford University Press).

Burnett, N., 2002, 'Working with the Private Sector in Primary and Middle School Education: Towards a Policy Framework,' draft, The World Bank SASHD, Washington DC.

Government of Pakistan, 2002, 'Pakistan Integrated Household Survey', Federal Bureau of Statistics, Islamabad.

Government of Pakistan, 1998, 'Education Sector Performance in the 1990s: Analysis from the PIHS', Federal Bureau of Statistics, Islamabad.

Gazdar, H., 1999, 'Universal Basic Education in Pakistan: Commentary on Strategy and Results of a Survey', SDPI Working Paper Series No. 39, Islamabad.

Government of Pakistan, 1999, *Economic Survey 1998-99*, Finance Division, Economic Advisor's Wing, Islamabad.

Hirschman, A. O., 1970, *Exit, Voice and Loyalty: Responses to Declines in Firms, Organizations, and States* (Cambridge, Massachusetts: Harvard University Press).

Hoodbhoy, P., 1998, 'Out of Pakistan's Educational Morass: Possible? How?' in ed. P. Hoodbhoy, *Education and the State: Fifty Years of Pakistan* (Karachi: Oxford University Press).

Kardar, S., 2001, 'Private Sector in Education', report prepared for the World Bank, Systems (Pvt.) Limited, Lahore.

Khan, A. H., 1998, 'Community Based Schools and the Orangi Project', in ed. P. Hoodbhoy, *Education and the State: Fifty Years of Pakistan* (Karachi: Oxford University Press).

Khan, S. R., 2001, 'Promoting Democratic Governance: The Case of Pakistan', *European Journal of Development Research*, Vol. 13, No. 2.

SAHE (Society for Advancement of Education), 1997, *Directory of NGOs in Education*, Lahore.

Stiglitz, J. E., 1998, 'Principal and Agent', in *Allocation, Information and Markets, The New Palgrave Dictionary of Economics and The Law*, ed. P. Newman (New York: Grove's Dictionaries), pp. 241-53.

TVO (Trust for Voluntary Organizations), 1994, *Directory of NGOs*, Prepared by Dataline Services, Islamabad.

UNDP, 2002, *Human Development Report*, and various years (New York: Oxford University Press).

World Bank, 1998, 'Pakistan: Public Expenditure Review: Reform Issues and Options', Report No. 18432-Pak, Islamabad.

Annex 2.1

Table 1. Parental qualifications across government, private, and NGO primary schools

Parental background/ school type	Government	Private	NGO
Mean education of father (years of schooling)	3.43 (2.2)	4.64 (2.44)	4.58 (2.29)
Mean education of mother (years of schooling)	1.89 (3.87)	2.59 (2.08)	2.53 (4.12)
Percentage of parents categorized as extremely poor@	13.9	5.4	5.1
Percentage of parents categorized as poor	52.1	26.3	29.7
Percentage of parents categorized as middle class	31.3	51.0	49.8
Percentage of parents categorized as rich	2.7	17.3	15.4

Source: SDPI survey, 1998.

Notes: Parentheses contain standard deviations.

@ The wealth index was based on the possession of durable goods and mode of transport. Since the computations run into two pages, the details are available on request.

Table 2.   Basic facilities across government, private, and NGO primary schools

(Percentages)

Facilities/school type	Government	Private	NGO
Desks available for students	40	60	84
Chairs available for students	44	81	95
Desks/chairs for teachers	74	81	97
Indoor classes	70	91	98
Electricity available	49	91	98
Fans in classrooms	33	86	93
Drinking water available	70	100	98
Washrooms available	40	95	100
Washrooms available clean	58	74	91
Maps and charts used	74	81	97
Models used for teaching	7	7	23
Library available	7	28	51

Source: SDPI survey, 1998.

Table 3.   Management policy across government, private, and NGO primary schools

(Percentages)

Policy/school type	Government	Private	NGO
Mean student absentee rate	6.1	10.1	5.4
	(15.3)	(20.1)	(12.4)
Schools expel chronic student absentees	42	26	26
Students beaten	48	47	37
Using own curriculum	2	46	52
Mother tongue as medium of instruction@	49	21	20
Multi-grade teaching	27	42	20
Regular inspections conducted	88	70	60
Have a school management committee	53	9	49
Mean monthly fees (Rs)#	2.9	120.7	107.9
	(4.1)	(73.4)	(49.2)
Poor students attend free	25	56	77
Parents checking homework	40	64	61
Report card shown to parents	33	91	89

Source: SDPI survey, 1998.
Notes: Parentheses contain standard deviations.
   @ = The alternative was the national language.
   # The exchange rate of the rupee (Rs) for the US $ was roughly 58 in mid-2003.

Table 4. Teacher characteristics across government, private, and NGO primary schools

Teacher characteristics/school type	Government	Private	NGO
Mean teacher salaries	3,567	1,800	2,317
	(1,537)	(2,379)	(2,339)
Mean teacher experience	9.95	7.58	4.47
	(5.8)	(17.2)@	(4.5)
In-service teacher training (%)			
None	47.6	92.7	53.5
Less than one month	16.7	2.4	14.0
One to two months	28.6	0.0	9.3
Two months or more	7.1	4.9	23.2
Teachers' educational qualifications (%)			
Middle (8 years)	0.0	7.1	0.0
Matric (10 years)	11.6	11.9	13.9
Intermediate (12 years)	46.5	47.6	37.2
Bachelors	25.6	23.8	37.2
Masters	16.3	9.5	11.6
Pre-service teacher training qualifications (%)*			
None	0.0	62.5	50.0
Junior Vernacular (JV)	2.3	5.0	0.0
Primary Teacher Certificate (PTC)	44.1	17.5	16.7
Certificate of Teaching (CT)	25.6	10.0	26.2
Bachelors Education (B. Ed.)	23.3	2.5	4.8
Masters Education (M. Ed.)	4.7	2.5	2.4
Other teacher characteristics			
Teachers provide extra help after school (%)	58	63	65
Teachers provide tuition after school (%)	12	26	30
Mean teacher absentee rates	11.7	10.7	5.9
	(15.0)	(16.3)	(6.1)

Source: SDPI survey, 1998.

Notes: Parentheses contain standard deviations.

@ = Four teachers had greater than twenty years experience.

* = The primary teacher certificate (PTC) is a nine-month vocational option after matriculation. Those wanting to teach middle school are required to earn a teachers' certificate (CT), which again entails nine months of training. The JV (Junior Vernacular) is the lowest level of pre-service teacher training qualification.

Annex 2.2: Case Studies

Case study No. 1: Good NGO school

School Type   :   NGO
Field team   :   Yasmin Khattak & Shahbaz Bokhari
Date   :   23 November 1998

This was the biggest middle girls' school in the area. The school had 700 students enrolled and twenty teachers.

Was the schooling successful?

Yes, very successful.

School factors

The school building was fully equipped with requisite teaching facilities. The school had a science laboratory which other schools in the area also made use of. All the teachers of the schools were well qualified and experienced. Most of the teachers received training from reputable teacher training centers, and they were well acquainted with modern teaching methods. Both the math and Urdu teachers performed well in the tests.

The performance of class 5 students in the tests was outstanding. Twenty-five per cent of the students secured 100 per cent marks in the Urdu test. It was evident that the administration gave proper attention to student confidence building.

Household factors

The student's socio-economic background was diverse and the parents of all the students were satisfied with the school's performance. Most of the families mentioned that they could not give time to their children's education at home but nonetheless the children were hardworking and managed on their own. The parents appreciated the school administration's efforts to keep them informed about their children's education.

Community factors

The community had full confidence in the school. They actively participated in school's activities. The school was built on land donated by the community. Two years after the establishment of the school, the school administration requested more land for a school laboratory and an examination hall, and the community once again donated the land. Although the material cost was provided by the NGO, the community contributed the labor costs.

The school had a strong school management committee (SMC) selected by the community. We were informed that the SMC had the power to remove a teacher or principal in consultation with the NGO. The SMC also handled absenteeism among students and if any student remained absent from school for more than six days, the school administration referred the case to the SMC. At the time of the field visit, the school was facing a congestion problem due to excess demand. With SMC concurrence, admissions were closed and the SMC was planning to approach the NGO's head office for more classrooms.

The community's willingness to allow an optimum utilization of the school building was commendable. There was no girls' college in the area, and so the community had allowed a private college to hold evening classes after school hours.

Case study No. 2: Poor NGO school

School Type   : NGO
Field team   : Sajid Kazmi & Saadia Almas
Date   : 29 September 1998

This school was started about seven years ago by the present principal who, with the help of some interested people, formed an NGO.

Was Schooling Successful?

No

School factors

The teacher's performance was abysmal (zero marks in math). The poor results of both the classes reflected poor teacher performance. Moreover, the school had not much space to accommodate even a very low number of students. Classes 1, 5 and 6 were housed in one room and only one teacher was teaching these three classes. Late fee payment was a big problem here. There were a number of students who had not paid their dues for over a year.

Household factors

The parents of all the students were farmers and almost all of them were financially sound. They viewed education to be the responsibility of the school authorities. In general, they seemed content with their children's performance. Perhaps some quietly protested by not paying the fee!

Community factors

According to the parents present in the community meeting, the school was doing well on a number of counts. According to them, small class sizes and discipline were plus points. Given the large population in the village, an alternative interpretation of small class sizes was also possible. Notwithstanding the parent's view of discipline, students skipped classes, and the school administration had asked the shopkeepers around the school to keep a lookout for such students and inform teachers about them. The parents also viewed the extra-curricular activities organized by the school as a mark of success. The school had a village education committee (VEC) comprising of parents, teachers, and notables of the village.

Case study No. 3: Good private school

School Type   : Private
Filed team   : Sajid Kazmi & Rehana Shahani Baloch
Date   : 30 October 1998

Although a cooperative society was formed for this school, it operated as a for-profit school. The cooperative committee was formed in 1980, and almost half its members had passed away and had not been replaced. It was a higher secondary school with separate school and college sections and had more than 2600 students and 132 teachers.

Was schooling successful?

Yes

School factors

Students secured good marks in both tests in both classes. Although the teachers helped a few students, yet they were capable of doing well on their own anyway. In response to a complaint from the field team, the principal explained that it was a language issue since the math test was not in the Sindhi language. The school was coeducational, but girls and boys were separated by curtains hung across the middle of the classrooms. Discipline seemed good and even the teachers wore uniforms. Besides delivering good education, the school administration emphasized character building. One example of such training was a self-service tuck shop that ran on the honor system. The school had well-equipped labs and a very rich library. The large number of teachers ensured a good teacher-student ratio for quality education.

Households factors

Since the fee was not very high as compared to the other private schools, it was affordable for average income families. The households visited were not very affluent, and very satisfied with the performance of their children. They appreciated the school's emphasis on moral values and also felt that there was no preferential treatment for the students from rich families. During school hours, eatables from outside the school were not allowed to avoid poor students feeling inferior.

Community factors

The community was all praise for the school. Even the administration of the nearby NGO school that we visited felt that it was delivering quality education. The community felt that the principal's educational background had much to do with this success. While there was no special concession for poor students, the school administration persuaded affluent people to finance the education of students from poor families. The community rated the school discipline very highly, and was of the view that discipline was necessary to ensure quality education.

Case study No. 4: Poor private school

School Type   :   Private
Field team   :   Yasmin Khattak & Shahbaz Bokhari
Date   :   18 December 1998

The school was established in 1988 but had a total of seventy students enrolled in all the classes.

Was the schooling successful?

No

School factors

Although the school had its own building, it was in a very poor condition. There were only three small classes that barely had the capacity of accommodating a maximum of fifteen students. However, thirty students were stuffed in these rooms and three classes were being held in each classroom. The students of both class 3 and class 5 performed very poorly in both the tests. The teacher could not attempt the math test and barely got 40 per cent marks in the Urdu test. The teachers were neither well-qualified nor well-trained.

Household factors

Most of the students belonged to well-off families. The fathers were educated but the mothers were mostly illiterate. During household visits, mothers indicated satisfaction with the school, but fathers viewed the school's educational standard to be poor. They did however express satisfaction with the attention paid by the school administration to discipline, and some indicated this to be their reason for opting for a private school.

Community factors

The community revealed in a focus group meeting that it was not satisfied with the performance of the school. They felt that while private schools generally perform better than government schools, this school was an exception. They revealed that the administration of this school bribed the examination authorities to pass all their students in class 5 to show a 'perfect' result. Once again, good discipline was highlighted as the singular achievement of this private school.

Case study No. 5: Good government school

School Type   : Government
Field team   : Rahat Almas & Shahbaz Bokhari
Date   : 30 September 1998

This school was established as a primary school in 1885, given the status of middle school in 1906 and finally upgraded to a high school in 1956. The high school was shifted to another building and the original building remained as the primary school. The primary school had 800 students and twenty-three teachers.

Was the schooling successful?

Yes, very successful

School factors

Although the school had nine rooms, these were insufficient to accommodate the large student body. Each class had three or four sections (twenty-two in all). Class 5 had 150 students with four sections. Eight classes were held in the verandas and eight classes were using the examination hall of the adjacent high school. Although there was a shortage of classrooms, student performance was outstanding.

The teaching staff seemed very hardworking and dedicated to their responsibilities. Most teachers were educated in the same school and an emotional attachment was evident. Teachers had the responsibility for a given section from class 1 all the way until class 5. Most students obtained over 80 per cent marks in both tests. Before we handed out the questionnaires, a lecture against cheating was delivered by the teacher.

Apart from the dedication of the teachers, another reason for the good performance was the high standard of education in the associated village high school. Admission to class 6 was by examination and competition was tough. The teachers of the primary school viewed getting their students admitted a matter of honor.

Household factors

The parents were unanimous is viewing this school as delivering a good education and also an exception among government schools. Many of them were ex-students of this school and proud to send their children to it. They pointed out that students come to this school from a distance of up to 15 kilometers. The parents also claimed to be giving due attention to their children's homework in view of the high expectations of the teachers.

Community factors

The education department trained the School Management Committee (SMC) members. Parents were given proper representation in the committee. To enable a long tenure on the committee, parents of children in the early classes were given preference. All committee members were old students of the headmaster and this was one reason why they actively contributed to the management of the school. SMC members spent some time informing us of cases of corruption in the education department.

The community as a whole also seemed interested and active. They made contributions on request and as a result the school had electricity. In general, the community was of the view that with the exception of schools such as this one, government schools should be handed over to the private sector.

Case study No. 6: Poor government school

School Type   : Government
Field team   : Sajid Kazmi and & Rehana Shahani Baloch
Date   : 21 November 1998

This school ran multiple shifts and we visited the second shift since the premise was used as a secondary section during the morning shift.

Was schooling successful?

No

School factors

There were no teachers in the school when we first arrived at the school. The teachers were supposed to arrive at 12:30 p.m., but came at 2:00 p.m. Students were playing in the playground when we arrived. Shortly after, the senior students assembled all the students in the playground and held the assembly, recited prayers, and sang the national anthem. It seemed as if this was their routine and the students confirmed that it was indeed the case. The students' results in both classes and for both tests were very poor. They had very poor test-taking abilities, lacked confidence, and seemed at a complete loss. There were three teachers and five classes. Teachers complained that they were short of teaching staff. They told us that this was a Sindhi school and they were not provided a Sindhi teacher. While the building was new, it was poorly maintained and already in a bad condition.

Household factors

The children came from very poor households. They told us that they could not afford to send their children to private schools or they would have done so. They were of the view that the private schools were delivering quality education because there was a proper monitoring system. They felt their children seemed dull and held the teachers responsible for this sorry state of affairs. They informed us that the headmaster took no interest in administering the school.

Community factors

The community was very unhappy with the school. The teachers routinely came late and paid no attention to the students. They didn't bother about the students not wearing uniforms or remaining absent for long periods. They complained about the lack of a proper monitoring system. We were informed that second-shift teachers had absolutely no chance of being caught out for neglect of duty because government offices closed at 2:00 p.m., and this school started at 1:00 p.m. Thus the teachers took full advantage of this lack of supervision. Most shocking, we were informed that the school was being used as gambling den and addicts remained in the school throughout the day. The teachers played cards during school hours while students were noisy and quarreled among themselves. As a result, the students were compelled to take private tuition from the teachers.

NOTES

1. Thanks are also due to Haris Gazdar for very useful comments on successive drafts and to Sajid Kazmi and Zainab Latif for assisting me in writing an earlier draft published in the *European Journal of Development Research* Vol. 17, No. 2, pp. 199-223, 2005.
2. A critical research issue is whether community participation induced or harnessed by development NGOs produces a higher quality product and sustainable service delivery at a competitive price. This issue is explored in chapter 3.
3. Interest in this subject has grown. Refer to Kardar (2001), Andrabi, Das, and Khwaja (2002), and Burnett (2002).
4. For a concise description refer to Stiglitz (1998).
5. The corporate scandals of 2002 in the USA show how difficult it is to align principal-agent interests.
6. Hirschman (1970).
7. Refer to chapter 1, section 1.5.

8. We constructed a wealth index based on durable goods and mode of transport possessed. By this criterion, 59 per cent of the children of government schools came from the most deprived households while this was true for 38 per cent of private and NGO schools. Again, while only 5 per cent of the children from government schools came from the wealthiest households, this was true for 23 per cent and 22 per cent of private and NGO school children. Thus the household wealth profile of the NGO and private school children was virtually identical and much higher than that of government school children (also refer to Annex 2.1, Table 1).

9. Refer to Khan (2001) for an account of devolution and education in Pakistan.

10. Refer to the introduction for definitions of 'non-government' schooling and for the relative size of the government, NGO, and private sectors.

11. Refer to chapter 1, section 1.4.3.

12. The differences in Table 2.1 may be due to household characteristics rather than the schools *per se*. As Annex 2.1, Table 1 indicates, NGO and private schools cater to the better-off rural households relative to government schools. This issue is quantitatively addressed in chapter 6.

13. Eleven per cent of the fathers and 27 per cent of the mothers of government school students were illiterate compared to 5 per cent each for NGO schools and 16 per cent and 18 per cent for private schools respectively. These numbers are way below the national average because they represent the response of parents of school children (randomly selected class 5 students). Also see Annex 2.1, Table 1.

14. Government of Pakistan (1998, p. 33).

15. The mean teacher salary and experience is reported in Annex 2.1, Table 4.

16. The mean salary of government school teachers of Rs 3567 was about equal to the mean monthly salary of unskilled workers (using a straight average of the daily wage for the national and four provincial capitals and multiplying by 30) and less than half the monthly salary of skilled workers like masons and carpenters. This information is based on Government of Pakistan, Statistical Supplement, (1999, p. 143)]. However, government teachers are entitled to benefits like a provident fund, health facilities and pension that are not accessible to daily-wage workers.

17. The lack of monitoring of government schools is often mentioned as a cause of poor performance. However, there was a mean of 4.23 (standard deviation, 2.78) inspections of government schools compared to 3.03 (s. d., 1.99) and 2.54 (s.d., 1.24) for private and NGO schools. Also see Annex 2.1, Table 3.

18. We generated a physical quality index based on the availability of the following: boundary wall, desks, chairs, *taats* (mats), indoor teaching, electricity, fans, drinking water, washrooms (both availability and quality) and library. Based on this, the quality score ranged from 0 to a maximum of 12. The mean score on this index for government, private and NGO schools was 5.2 (s.d., 2.71), 9.0 (s.d., 1.49) and 10.1(s.d., 1.16) respectively. Also see Annex 2.1, Table 2.

19. See Annex 2.1, Table 4 for teacher characteristics in a comparative context.

20. Only four out of the forty-three private schools had a PTA (parent-teacher association) or SMC (school management committee) while this was the case for twenty-nine government schools (mandatory) and twenty-two NGO schools (optional). Parents were represented in no government schools' SMC/PTAs and in only 9 per cent of NGO SMCs/PTAs. Refer to Annex 2.1, Table 3 and for more details to chapter 3.

21. See Annex 2.1, Table 3 for the mean monthly fees.

56 BASIC EDUCATION IN RURAL PAKISTAN

22. While it may be difficult to justify subsidizing a commercial activity, the government could ensure that tax authorities do not harass private schools as seems to be happening according to press reports. Also refer to chapter 4, section 4.2, on the issue of private sector subsidies.

23. It was difficult to find a completely consistent pattern for parental involvement in schooling across the three types of schools. Sometimes, very educated parents were complaisant about very poor private sector schooling as though they had done the best by their children and need not worry further. While the poor and illiterate were generally unaware and disinterested, they sometimes complained vociferously about the poor service delivery of government schools.

24. For an account of NGO schooling in general refer to Baqir (1998), and for a specific example of community-based schooling to A. H. Khan (1998). The names of the schools have been changed to ensure anonymity.

25. World Bank (1998).

3 [1]

Participation and Collective Action in Basic Education in Government and NGO Schools

3.1. Introduction

The Participatory Development Program (PDP) was included as part of the Social Action Plan discussed in chapter 1. Initially fourteen projects were funded in 1996 (for a two-year period) based on the principle of community participation and sixteen projects were selected for the second phase. If community participation makes the difference, then the PDP, while a laudatory attempt, was a small one. Our contention is that contracting out a few pilot projects to be executed in a participatory manner is an ineffective way of achieving participation in schooling.

A better approach is to investigate which of the key aspects of participation and collective action work for a particular sector. Since our focus is on basic education in the rural sector, the relevant question for us is which of these principles can be readily applied to all rural schooling projects or what is it that impedes participation?

It is true that SAP's concern with participation went beyond the PDP. SAP encouraged community participation in site selection, hiring of local female teachers, and on-going community participation via school management committees (SMCs) or parent teacher associations (PTAs). This is, in fact, the most effective way of introducing community participation in schooling. These committees, consisting of teachers, parents, and local notables were vested with managerial and financial powers. How effective these efforts were is investigated in this chapter. In addition, we explore how effectively NGO schools incorporate participation in their functioning relative to public sector schools.[2]

This chapter is based on three major sources of information. The first includes field-visit interviews with school staff, members of (SMCs/PTAs), government line department officials, NGO members, educationists and donor organization members, and a review of documents and reports. The second source is an extensive review of the literature. The third is the field survey used for this book, described in Appendix 1, that included an exploration of government and NGO SMCs/PTAs. The findings from the three sources are broadly consistent and reinforce each other, although findings from the sample survey are more negative than those emerging from the field visits and the literature review. Our focus, as in the rest of the book, is on rural areas, although the field visits included urban schools and the lessons carry over.

In section 2, we present a conceptual framework that sets the context for participation in education. In section 3, we present an evaluation of how SMCs/PTAs functioned based on the three sources cited above. We end with a summary.

3.2. Conceptual issues

The collective action framework is the broad area within which to view community participation.[3] In this regard, education has some special features. In the general case, Olsen (1971) showed that, due to the free-rider problem, collective action was likely only if the benefits to any one individual were enough to offset the total costs to the community from some particular action. Applying this theory to rural water supply in Pakistan, Khan (1999) showed that collective action or participation in rural water supply schemes is likely if objective conditions dictate that marginal benefits will be close to marginal costs for most individuals. As it turned out, in many cases, this held true since a uniform tariff was applied to all villagers and the nature of many water supply schemes was such that all had potentially equal benefits.

Education is a more complicated case of participation and collective action. First, not all members of the village stand to directly benefit from the school. The direct benefits are likely to accrue only to those parents whose children or relatives are currently in the school. Second, the beneficiaries are not a stable population as in the case of rural water supply or health. When a particular child successfully completes primary school, the parents or relatives of that child are no longer direct beneficiaries. Of course, the whole community is an indirect beneficiary in that better quality schools add to the reputation of the community and will at least provide a valuable service to future generations if not current children or relatives.

Given this special nature of education, from whom should we expect participation? Our contention is that, since parents have most at stake and since the size of the parent-teacher committee needs to be limited for effectiveness, the most interested parents should be on the committees. Teachers should naturally be on the committees as the key agents in delivering education. If we are right, we really should be concerned with PTAs rather than SMCs on prior grounds. This does not preclude cash, kind or labour contributions from the community, but it gives the parents precedence in overseeing school affairs. However, given Pakistan's political and cultural milieu, one then has to address the issue of local notables or influential members of the community who would be excluded.

The role of notables is a complex one. In most cases, their presence on the SMC is merely a formality. They generally have no direct personal stake in the school or any deep interest in education. However, as prominent members of the community, they have to be represented in all community matters. In some cases, their presence on a SMC may merely allow them to appropriate resources that might become available. However, there are also situations in which they may take a charitable interest in the school and contribute to it financially. Thus, conceptually, having them on the SMC amounts to involving a potential sponsor. Our view is that while the notables sometimes play a benign role, the potential for harm is greater and relying on them to play the parent's role is not advisable. Thus, we knowingly endorse the concept of a PTA rather than a SMC since it emphasizes the greater role for parents. However, given the local power of notables, the state would have to run interference to ensure parents rather than notables have a voice in overseeing school affairs.

Only a few of the prospective parents will volunteer to be elected to PTAs.[4] Thus, education is even a more restricted case of collective action than implied above by the 'shifting constituency' of parents as students graduate from school and new ones join. In fact, 'free-riding' is built into PTA supervision since parents not doing anything will benefit from the good efforts of those on the PTA. This is true the world over and this participation relies more on the civic sense and voluntarism of a few dedicated individuals rather than on the collective efforts of the community or even the concerned parents as a body. Support NGOs and donors who have a 'one size fits all' perception of participation may end up being surprised about how little the standard model applies in this case.

One needs to be cautious about the role specified for rural parents in school affairs. However, in spite of illiteracy or low education levels, parents are capable of playing the monitoring role. This would include ensuring that the school's physical structure and facilities are well maintained and conducive to learning, teachers and students are punctual and interested, corporal punishment is eliminated, and that finances are in order. Developing these capabilities should be the role that training should play. Expecting rural parents to play a part in pedagogy or syllabus development would be unrealistic and such training may be wasted for the time being.

We are then left with the question of how to make the participation of the parents on the PTA effective? This has everything to do with the power dynamics on the PTA and little to do with devolution of powers to the local administration.[5] Devolution and empowerment of local government has much going for it in other circumstances, but is not the key to good parental supervision. In chapter 2 we report that the major problem in effective parental supervision was the lack of power parents have relative to teachers or educational officials. If parents are to be effective, teachers have to have an incentive to listen to them. This is a key issue in effective parental participation that we will return to later.

3.3. Evaluation of SMCs/PTAs[6]

3.3.1. Field visits

Based on the lessons learnt from SAPP I (Social Action Plan Project, Phase I) community participation emerged as a key strategy for SAPP II. The design for community participation in the education sector is based on institutionalizing the interaction between the community and school through the establishment of the school management committees or parent teacher associations (SMCs/PTAs). This incorporated social mobilization, financial empowerment, and management training of SMCs/PTAs with a focus on enabling parents and community members to play a key role in the management of primary and middle schools. The community, in theory, emerged as a major stakeholder in ensuring that services work for them. The operational plans of all the provinces include descriptions of the objectives, functions, procedures, modalities, activities, and targets that pertain to the establishment and operation of the SMCs.

The formal notification for the formation/reconstitution of SMCs and PTAs was issued simultaneously in all provinces in 1994 as a critical step for ensuring community participation in the implementation of SAPP I. There were several problems with the government notifications. First, the statutory inclusion of non-parents (notables) into the committee, who may or may not be genuine stakeholders, and, as such, may be able to subvert the functioning of the committees to suit their own agendas, is problematic as explained in the conceptual framework. Representation on the committee should be at the discretion of the committee members rather than imposed as a statutory requirement. Second, a teacher or head teacher should be explicitly ruled out as the chairperson of the committee since there is a conflict of interest in their assuming such a role. Third, the expectation of fund-raising by the committees is excessive and unrealistic. Finally, for the Punjab, the reporting requirements are onerous and not all are necessary.

On the one hand, it appears that where community involvement was ensured prior to the establishment of schools, as has been the case for new schools established under the community support process in Balochistan, NWFP, and Sindh, there is greater participation by the community in the functioning of the schools. On the other hand, the official notification of forming SMCs/PTAs by the government in existing schools has resulted in a group of nominated individuals, with little interest in the running of the school, assuming a representative role. It has also led to minimal representation of parents, and a general resentment by teachers of a body perceived by them as having been set up for supervising and monitoring their performance. The repeated reconstitution of SMCs, giving increasing authority to parents, drew an angry response from teachers' associations in the Punjab who resorted to strikes, protests, and even legal action against the education department. The fault also lies with the aggressive media strategy adopted by the government in promoting the role of the community without taking the teachers' unions into confidence.

The parents' role in management can be effective in ensuring that the schools are functioning and the teachers are doing their job. It is also possible for them to provide some minimal support in the form of labor, materials and funds. As earlier stated, the majority of parents are not literate and so it is not possible for them to monitor the quality of education in terms of its pedagogical content and other aspects of quality. However, they can judge if the teachers are punctual and the child is well-treated and given due educational attention. Even so, poverty is likely to result in decreased participation of communities in the education of their children as parents struggle to make a living.

The importance of having communities and parents take an interest in the local school has emerged from the failure of education departments and their field staff to provide functioning government schools (see chapter 2). This has resulted in high dropout and low retention of children at the primary level (see chapter 1). The role of parents/communities is essentially a minimalist one of ensuring that teachers are present and education is taking place. However, there is a difference in how the provincial departments of education, teachers, NGOs, communities and parents perceive the role of SMCs/PTAs. There is also a difference in perception and actual practice.

The government of General Musharraf instituted a devolution reform that in principle can mean a greater role for the community and parents in the management of schools. NGOs also perceive the formation of SMCs/PTAs and parental involvement as a move towards devolution of authority with the SMCs/PTAs becoming more influential and empowered in determining the quality of education and school management. However the department of education and teachers prefer the SMC/PTA to channel material help in the form of repairs, construction, and maintenance to the schools as well as funds.

In Balochistan, in schools opened under the community support process (CSP), the post of a teacher was seen as a village asset and was accepted as such by parliament. Thus, the teacher had to be local and his/her appointment had to take place according to established criteria including his/her selection and appointment by the PTA. NGOs were contracted to initiate the CSP based on fourteen steps for opening a community school. Empowerment of communities, as understood by NGOs in this province, meant involving them in opening schools and building their capacities in school administration, management and financial affairs, ensuring the regular attendance of the local teacher and advocating for the right to quality education of their children with the government. The empowerment component needs to be built in more consciously as the government's perception of community participation is to shift the burden of education on to communities without giving them the right to question line departments on their performance.

The role of the department of education and their field staff, comprising thousands of male and female education officers and learning coordinators, also needs to be reviewed in the changed scenario of community participation. It is quite clear that the field staff rarely performs assigned duties. To be effective, the field staff needs to carry out field supervision and be accessible to the SMCs/PTAs and communities.

The teacher and his/her role is critical for quality education, but it also is generally out of the purview of the community, which can only put moral pressure on the teacher to attend school but is not in a position to remove or replace him/her. The community can appoint additional or supplementary teachers from its' own resources if necessary. The community can also arrange teacher training but cannot compel the teacher to participate in the training or to implement it in the classroom. The community can ensure that the teacher is local if a new school is being opened, but it cannot do much with existing teachers or with political interference in postings and transfers.

The initial focus of SMCs/PTAs has been on ensuring that funds allocated for classroom consumables and petty repairs are deposited in bank accounts opened by communities and are, in reality, spent on the items for which they have been earmarked. Training of SMCs/PTAs in accessing those funds and utilizing them is, therefore, the first step. However, even before this, provincial governments' finance departments and departments of education need to develop simple mechanisms with clearly identified rules and regulations for the disbursement of these funds.

The SAPP-II Education Core Reform Program and Core Reform Program Monitoring Indicators for each province were explicit on the community participation component. These included, for example, the number of active PTAs as demonstrated by the involvement of fathers and mothers in school related procurements (annual repairs and educational materials) and facilitation of school operations. The means of verification for these include directorate of primary education records of money transferred in non-lapsable grants to PTAs and post-audit documents, reports of PTA training programs including registers of attendance and reports of Third Party Monitoring. All the indicators relate to the PTAs and/or release of funds, and not to the need for training and capacity building of departments of education as well as other concerned departments, such as the finance departments, whose understanding of devolution is critical to their acceptance of SMCs/PTAs handling funds.

All provincial finance departments were reluctant to release funds to the divisional or district level. In their perception, even the district education officers (DEOs) were not professionally trained to handle funds. The SMCs/PTAs were viewed with great suspicion and the conviction was widespread that they would misuse the money released to them.

3.3.2. Literature review

In the literature on education reform, parental and community participation is only one aspect of decentralization and there is a limited focus on it. Much of the experimentation with decentralization has been in Latin America and part IV of the book edited by Randall and Anderson (1999) provides a comprehensive account of it. Other accounts of various dimensions of decentralizations include Jimenez and Sawada (1998), King and Özler (1998), King and Orazem (1999), Di Gropella (1999), Eskeland (2000), Winkler and Gershberg (2000), and Grootaert, Oh, and Swamy (2002).[7]

Important studies on the state of SMCs/PTAs and their training in Pakistan include World Bank (1996), Government of Punjab/MSU (1998), Bunyad (1998), International Institute of Education et al. (1998), Merchant (1999), Khan and Haque (1999), Beckley (1999), Elahi (1999), British Council (1999), Hussein (1999) and MSU (n.d.).

Elahi (1999, p. 11) pointed out that notification of DEOs to form PTAs in Sindh was sudden and the action precipitous, so much so, that many parents who did not even know what a PTA was, were suddenly members. The sub-section above and the results of the national survey in the next two sub-sections indicate a similar story for the other provinces. Since little was hence achieved, this created a credibility problem for NGOs who were later contracted. Interviews indicated that donors, anxious for target achievement and disbursements, pushed the process and in this regard were equally culpable.

Bunyad (1998) did a useful descriptive review of PTAs in fifty-one schools across nine districts of the NWFP. The researchers reported hurriedly constituted PTAs with no capacity building, confusion caused by multiple notifications, constant change in membership partly due to teacher transfers, a lack of understanding of the basic concept of a PTA on the part of all concerned, no understanding of roles and responsibilities, no training, no monitoring and evaluation system, neglect of the gender issue, no follow-up by the directorate of primary education, no co-operation among DEOs and NGOs, political interference in the formation and activities of the PTA and no training for the education department in community participation in order to handle this complex task. More disturbing, there was no parental involvement or contribution and teachers were operating accounts as sole signatories.

The results of the survey indicate that the NGOs engaged in more community mobilization, created greater awareness among teachers and to some extent among parents. There were elections for membership among a sizeable number of schools, all PTAs had a bank account and all PTA members contributed to it. Even so, NGO-established PTAs were not engaging in systematic training and there was a lack of clarity about roles and responsibilities. While there was virtually no activity among government-established PTAs, NGO-established PTAs were meeting regularly. However, even NGOs hurriedly conducted school functions in anticipation of the study team's visit.

While there was no evidence of an improvement in teacher attendance, there was evidence that PTAs were engaging in collective activity such as contribution to building boundary walls, erecting sunshades and making financial contribution for electrification. Such collective action even pre-dated the formation of PTAs indicating that the potential for collective action is there. There were also some negative findings such as the use of false expectations about financial assistance as a motivational factor and deterring mother's participation using the pretext of cultural norms.

The study by the Government of Punjab/MSU (1998) is probably the most comprehensive and based on a stratified random sample of 175 schools in Gujranwala and 150 in D. G. Khan. An important objective of the study was to identify the success of the massive training program designed to cover 65,000 members via the training of master trainers. Parents, particularly mothers, were under-represented on the SMCs while influentials were over-represented. The interaction of the department of education officials and SMC members was very limited and, in many cases, committee members were teacher's relatives. At the time of the survey, training had not been received by

two-thirds of the D. G. Khan SMCs and two-fifths of the Gujranwala
SMCs. Also, the training was directed only at the head teacher and to
a lesser extent to the other teachers. Only one-fifth of the SMCs in
D. G. Khan and 6 per cent in Gujranwala received the training booklets
on SMC management and procurements. Just over a quarter of the
SMCs in D. G. Khan and no SMC in Gujranwala received government
funds. However, most of the SMCs that received funds (88 per cent)
maintained accounts and reported them to the members.

The activities the SMCs engaged in included committee meetings,
visits to schools, meeting parents, teachers, heads and students,
reviewing attendance registers, financial support to students and talking
to mosque *imams* (prayer leader). The objective of this activity was to
increase enrollments, reduce dropout rates, and contain absenteeism.
The results of their analysis showed that training does seem to
contribute to marginally higher activity levels. Also, female's
representation on committees, government funding, and access to
training booklets was associated with higher activity levels.

MSU (n.d., p. 6) also cites results of surveys to indicate that most
SMCs tried to fulfil their functions, met at least once in the year prior
to the surveys, visited schools, and households and had meetings with
teachers, parents and students, took steps to raise enrollment rates and
reduce dropout rates, checked attendance registers, supported students
financially, and took steps to improve the classroom environment.
There was however no meaningful interaction with the department of
education and few took measures to improve teacher attendance.

Merchant (1999) reports on similar blanket notification of PTAs for
Sindh schools as was the case in NWFP and the Punjab. In 1998, with
UNICEF support, 5325 PTAs were to be trained. The training modules
and manuals were developed for the purpose. In all, the author notes
that 7000 PTAs were trained, many with the department of education's
efforts by using department officials (resource persons, learning
coordinators, and supervisors) as master-trainers. A one-day orientation
workshop for department officials in July 1999 in Sindh highlighted
some interesting issues. They perceived that there was a lack of clarity
concerning their role, capture of PTAs by head teachers, political
interference that included take over attempts by the government
appointed *khidmat* (service) committees, fake PTAs chasing funds, and
educational officials demanding bribes to issue checks.

In May 1998, Rs 423 million were allocated to about 26,914 PTAs.
A study commissioned by the British Council Project Management

Office (1999) reported that the allocation was based on poor SEMIS (Sindh Education Management Information System) data, flaws in the formula for calculating grants, and multiple administrative layers for processing grants. Recommendations were directed at reforming and rationalizing the grant delivery system. Also, Hussein (1999, p. 9) pointed out that there was a need for allowing more flexibility in expenditures to meet real needs identified by the committees.

Hussein (1999) made some interesting observations regarding SMCs/PTAs. She pointed out that the autonomy of the Punjab and Sindh SMCs/PTAs is compromised by mandating the head teacher to also be the chairperson of the SMC/PTA.[8] While Sindh PTAs have a greater representation of parents on the PTA, their role regarding monitoring teacher performance is left ambiguous. The PTA is required to play a supportive role with an over-emphasis, because of the lack of balance, on purchasing and school infrastructure. While the role of the SMC has been spelt out for Punjab SMCs, it has created resentment among teachers and parents don't have any real implementing authority. However, if the department does take parent's complaints seriously, there is indirect authority but the problem of the head teacher as chairperson remains.[9] Balochistan PTAs suffer from both parents feeling un-empowered and teachers feeling resentful. Reservations about PTAs in NWFP were cited earlier, but quarterly reports from Khwendo Kor (1999) provides an interesting accounts of what PTAs can achieve working with communities.

The literature review essentially confirmed the findings based on field visits. The PTA/SMC formations were precipitous, so much so, parents on the committees were not aware of their existence. NGO-formed PTAs met more regularly, but even they often showed poor performance. There was an over-representation of notables on committees and an under-representation of women. Much of the training was directed at the head teacher who was often the most influential member of the PTA and hence not likely to monitor himself. Very few SMCs had training booklets though those that did had somewhat higher activity levels. Political interference in the functioning of SMCs/PTAs was rife. The allocation of funds was often based on flawed data and there was an overemphasis on purchases and school infrastructure. While studies suggested SMCs appeared to be performing many of the assigned functions, interaction with the department of education was inadequate and little was done about teacher absenteeism.

3.4. Results of a national sample survey

Data for the study was collected through extensive fieldwork carried out on 139 schools in the Punjab, Sindh, Balochistan, the NWFP and the Northern Areas between September and December 1998 and is described in Appendix 1. In this kind of paired sampling, the randomness extends to the selection of government schools. Twenty-one, four and twenty-two of the forty-three NGO, private and government schools included in the sample had a SMC or PTA respectively. There was only one female SMC in the eighty-six government and NGO schools visited.

We have presented the results of this survey regarding the SMCs/PTAs in two parts. The first part presents the qualitative findings of the field teams that engaged the communities, parents and PTA/SMC members in focus group meetings. In addition, they held meetings with the administrators of the sample area. Based on these meetings and observations, a field report was written on the night of the field visit. The field team also gave a structured questionnaire to the SMC/PTA. While this was the main source of information on SMCs/PTAs, a few questions on community participation and SMCs/PTAs were also fielded to households, communities, and teachers. The results of the analysis of the data generated from these questions are also reported below.

3.4.1. Field team qualitative evaluation

The status of school management committees (SMCs) in government schools was a disaster. Parents and the communities were usually oblivious of their existence, particularly in Sindh, where they were referred to as PTAs. If the presence of the PTA was common knowledge, they still happened to be non-functional. In many cases, the committees were stacked with the headmaster's relatives, friends, and retired teachers and had no parents on them. In a couple of cases, committee decisions were entirely made by a notable or a politician. For one school, a politician nominated six members, all from outside the village and, naturally, they did not bother to meet. Teacher interaction with parents was minimal and hostile. In one case, poor parents pointed out that their complaints were met with a rejoinder that they are welcome to withdraw their children. Middle class parents however met with more civil responses.

Generally, teachers viewed parent's involvement via the SMC/PTA as a threat and as an interference in their affairs, and they therefore refused to call such meetings. In one case in Kharan, Balochistan, the teachers actually turned abusive when parents dared to approach them to complain about the poor education their children were receiving.

Teachers had other reasons not to be thrilled about SMCs/PTAs. In one case, the teachers were expected to bribe the auditor to get a clear audit report, and so they merely allowed the allocated SMC funds to lapse. In at least two cases, teachers claimed that they took a collection to pay for utility bills and supplies.

Teacher recalcitrance was a major reason for the non-functionality of SMCs/PTAs. However, parental illiteracy (resulting in parents getting intimidated), poverty (such that survival concerns were of foremost importance to parents), suspicion (that teachers were misappropriating SMC/PTA funds)[10] and the lack of time (parents felt they had limited time and that education was the school's responsibility) were other important reasons for SMC/PTA non-functionality. In one focus group meeting, parents expressed the view that if they are to serve on such committees, they should be paid for the time they put in.

However, SMCs/PTAs were not always completely ineffective. In some cases, it was obvious that the members had been trained and in one case the register for minutes was meticulously maintained. In other cases, the SMC/PTA was a vehicle to collect donations from communities for needed infrastructure such as boundary walls, water tanks, a new branch of the school or new classrooms, furniture, and repairing a hand-pump.[11] The lack of clarity in the SMC's objectives was perceived to be a problem. In one community, the same notables were on the SMC of both government and NGO schools, and they were much more active in working for the NGO school since they had a much clearer sense of what was expected from them.

Only one out of the forty-three government schools had a functioning SMC. The education department trained the members of the SMC. Parents were given proper representation in the committee. To enable a long tenure on the committee, parents of children in the early classes were given preference. All the committee members were old students of the head master and this was one reason why they actively worked for the management of the school. Despite this special reason for parents to feel involved, this case indicated that it is possible to have functioning and effective SMCs, with involved parents, in the government sector.[12]

3.4.2. Quantitative analysis[13]

We start here with an overall self-assessment by government and NGO schools of their SMCs on a four-point scale of 'poor' to 'very good'. The question put to the committees was 'rate how well do you think the SMC is doing in managing the school?' Eighty-six per cent (25) government SMCs rated themselves as 'poor' or 'fair' while only one rated itself as 'good'. By contrast, 77 per cent NGO SMCs rated themselves as 'good' or 'very good' and only 18 per cent rated themselves as 'fair'. No NGO SMC rated itself as 'poor'. It is naturally a cause of much concern why government SMC self-assessment is so poor, particularly when an outside evaluation tends to be much harsher.

The motivation for forming SMCs could be an indicator of collective action and hence community maturity. We therefore inquired about who instigated the formation of SMCs for NGO schools. In 82 per cent NGO schools (18), the idea was that of the NGO and only in one case was it that of the community. SMCs are now mandatory in government schools and so the more interesting question was why only two-thirds (29) of the government schools sampled had SMCs?

On the face of it, SMCs did seem to be important in managing the school. About four-fifths of government schools that had SMCs (23) and 96 per cent of such NGO schools (21) reported that the SMC managed the schools. Government school SMCs had more members such that about three-fourths of them (22) had nine or more members. For NGO schools, only about one-fourth (5) had nine or more members. Again, on the face of it, a larger membership could mean more representation of the community. Thus the more important question about membership was not the numbers involved but the composition.

Nine-tenths of all SMC members in government schools were teachers. In fact, parents were not represented on a single committee! The parental representation on NGO SMCs was higher at 9 per cent, but even this was disappointing. Also, in four-fifths of such cases, parents continued on the committee even when their child left the school. Teachers at 86 per cent again represented the bulk of the representation on the SMCs. This says very little for actual community or parent participation in running schools. This is more so the case since in half the cases the NGO decided who would be represented on the committee and their representative was perceived to be the most influential on the committee. One could take heart from the fact that in over one-fourth of the cases (6), NGOs sought the consensus of the community in appointing parents to the SMC. Also, most in the focus group discussions claimed that those not on the SMC's got some say in decision-making in both NGO and government schools.

The NGO SMCs met more frequently. About nine-tenths of them (17) reported meeting at least once a month, while 55 per cent (16) government SMCs reported meeting only once a month and the rest (13) reported meeting every other month or less.

There were some interesting commonality and differences in the perceived functions of the NGO and government SMCs. Ensuring teacher attendance, student attendance, student discipline, and adequate training and supplies were perceived as SMC functions by a much larger number of NGO committees compared to the government committees. The only function in which there was parity was with regard to the proper maintenance of the school. About 86 per cent (19) NGO committees and 83 per cent government committees viewed this to be a function of the SMC. Thus government school SMCs had a rather limited perception of their role and this needs to be modified.

Ensuring prompt payment of fees by parents was a concern for 73 per cent (16) of NGO SMCs compared to about a third (10) of government SMCs. This is not surprising, since NGOs are much more dependent on fees for their financial sustainability than government schools. Teacher absenteeism was not perceived to be a problem in any NGO SMC and was noted to be a problem by one government SMC. Given that SMCs were predominantly composed of teachers, a biased response on teacher absenteeism is inevitable. Similarly, student absenteeism was reported to be problem by 14 per cent (4) government SMCs and by 23 per cent NGO SMCs (5). Both government (three out of four cases) and NGO (all cases) SMCs claim to have had substantial success in dealing with this problem by talking to the students and approaching relatives.

The greatest obstacle NGO SMCs claimed to face in performing their functions smoothly was a lack of funds (9) followed by a lack of parental co-operation (3). Over one-fifth (5) claimed to be facing no obstacle. While a similar number of government SMCs claimed to be facing no problems, 31 per cent (9) complained about the lack of co-operation from other teachers. Thus, taking teachers into confidence is of vital importance in government SMC training.

Forty-one per cent (9) NGO SMCs claimed to have received some training and all of them found it to be of value. Similarly, 38 per cent (11) government SMCs claimed to have received some training and 73 per cent (8) of those receiving training found it to be of value. The important question was why 62 per cent government SMCs received no training as they were supposed to?

As indicated earlier, there were also some questions regarding the SMC included in the household survey of 10 per cent students. Eighty per cent households who sent their child to an NGO school claimed there was a high parent-teacher interaction and half the households viewed the teachers to be responsive. For private and government schools, the statistics for parent-teacher interaction were 60 per cent and 76 per cent respectively, and for teacher responsiveness 30 and 39 per cent respectively.

Only 8 per cent (18) households (222) of children who went to government schools were aware that there was an SMC in the village. Of these, eight felt that the SMC did have an impact on the quality of education of the children. However, seven of these eight served on the SMC. By contrast, 15 per cent (33) households (221) of children going to NGO schools were aware of the SMC and 61 per cent (20) thought the SMC was effective.

The relevant questions in the community questionnaire also showed that the NGO social mobilization had a very limited impact in engendering community participation. Thus while twenty-eight communities claimed to have made some contribution of land for the NGO school relative to 21 per cent for the government school (mandatory), in three-fourths of these cases, the contribution came from a notable. Similarly, while nine communities claimed to have made contributions to the NGO school, relative to four for the government school, in two-thirds of these cases, the contribution came from a notable. About two-thirds of NGO schools ran a deficit and in only two cases was the community responsible for covering this. Also, only in one-quarter of all NGO schools did the SMC or community run the bank account, which was the same for government schools. While only two communities engaged in collective efforts to enroll children in government schools, only five did so for NGO schools. Thus, it appears that NGOs have concentrated more on running schools and less on mobilizing communities to participate in managing the schools themselves.

Summary

We found that there has certainly been much activity regarding the establishment and training of (SMCs/PTAs) even though little has been achieved across the four provinces. Even so, at least the basic infrastructure for participation has been established which could be improved and built upon.

As things stand, the constitution of the SMCs/PTAs has in most cases been via sudden notification, so much so, that many parents who had no idea what a PTA represents became members overnight. The repeated re-constitution of these committees to enhance the role of parents without taking teachers into confidence created resentment among teachers. Even if teachers were taken into confidence, there is little reason to believe that they would welcome an additional layer of monitoring so close to home, particularly if it is by parents they consider their intellectual and social inferiors.

If participation of parents via SMCs were to make any progress, it would have to be accompanied by several concomitant changes. First, teachers' attitudes would have to be slowly and painstakingly changed so that they really do view parents as partners in the education of their children. Second, the incentive structures would have to be changed so that the teachers have a reason to listen to parents. Thus teachers' increments and promotions would have to be partly dependent on parents' assessment of teacher performance at least in terms of punctuality and good treatment of the children. The government officials have to accept the importance of this parental input and be welcoming of and responsive to this input. Finally, the training of SMCs/PTAs, in order to enable them to perform their mandated tasks, must accompany these changes. Thus, while we put training at the end of a sequence of changes that are necessary, the current fixation on training pushes it without the accompanying public sector reform that is needed. We feel that the current political scenario, with its focus on devolution, is more likely to achieve such public sector reform.

Instead of the kind of empowerment mentioned above that is needed, both in Sindh and the Punjab, the head teacher is mandated to be the chair of the committees. Thus the parents have little autonomy. In the Punjab, there is at least a mechanism for hearing parental complaints in the government line department. However, with the head teacher as the chair, there is little chance of such complaints being passed up. Also, research shows that line department officials manifest complete disinterest and lack of interaction with communities and committees. Just as teachers must have an incentive to listen to parents so must the line department officials. Thus the evaluation of line department officials must similarly be partially based on parents' assessment of their efforts to work with them and committees to improve schooling.

There is much that needs to be done for improving educational administration. Even line department officials reported numerous wrongdoings. Fake SMCs/PTAs were drawing funds, the process of issuing grants was susceptible to political interference and line department officials were demanding bribes to release grants. Research also showed that the basis of making allocations still needs much fine tuning to avoid misallocations and flexibility and committee discretion would be desirable in order for real needs to be met. Also, the SMC/PTA fixation with acquisition of school materials seems totally misplaced. Their major focus should be on working with teachers to improve attendance of students and teachers, reducing corporal punishment, co-curricula activities, and other ways of generating greater interest in teaching and learning.

The documents and reports on this subject suggest that NGOs are more prone to engage in the kind of social mobilization that may change community and teachers' attitudes in the way desired. However, the scale of the task is so vast that these efforts do not amount to much. Also, even NGO initiated SMCs/PTAs show only relatively better performance than the SMCs/PTAs initiated by government educational department officials. While there is virtually no activity in most of the government formed SMCs/PTAs, at least the NGO formed committees were meeting regularly. However, the literature shows that, with some exceptions, they have not engaged in systematic training and even when NGOs have been contracted to form SMCs/PTAs, there has been a lack of clarity about roles and responsibilities among the various stakeholders.

The other factors that have a positive impact on SMC/PTA activity include having mothers represented on the committees. One study found that the presence of mothers on committees was associated with lower dropouts from the school. Much needs to be done on this score since, in the Punjab, mothers had representation on committees in less than one-fifth of the schools. Another factor that was shown to be positively associated with enhanced activity levels was access to good training booklets. Several training initiatives have produced good resource material that could now be adapted to local conditions and more widely disseminated.

The results of our survey, for the most part, confirmed and reinforced the findings from the first two sets of sources. First, only two-thirds of the schools in the sample had committees even though it is now mandatory to have them. Second, parents were not represented on any of the government school committees and there was parental representation on only 9 per cent of NGO school committees. This is a very serious problem since, conceptually, true participation in education requires, most of all, the involvement of concerned parents. Third, 86 per cent government school SMCs/PTAs rated their performance as 'poor' (compared to a 77 per cent self-assessment of NGO schools as 'good' or 'very good'). Over half of them were meeting less than once a month (compared to nine-tenths of NGO schools committees meeting at least once a month) and the incidence of non-functionality was very high. Fourth, despite all the claims of the extensive training underway, less than two-fifths claimed to have received any training. Finally, the fixation on repair and maintenance stood out in perception as the purpose of SMCs/PTAs. About 86 per cent NGO school committees and 83 per cent government school committees viewed the proper maintenance of the school as an important function of the committee. Many more NGO school committees viewed ensuring teacher attendance, student attendance, student discipline and adequate supplies as part of their role.

On the positive side, even prior to the formation of the SMCS/PTAs, the communities had been engaging in collective action. Thus, via collections, they had built boundary walls and provided water and electricity for the school. Thus, the raw potential for collective action is certainly there. Harnessing this potential is the real challenge.

References

Beckley, S. M., 1999, 'Communities as Partners in Education for Development', presented in the Sindh Primary Education Development, Government of Sindh/British Council Conference on Enhancing Capabilities for Community Participation—Revisiting Practices in Education Development, Karachi.

Bunyad, 1998, 'Third Party Evaluation of Parent-Teacher Associations of the Government of NWFP Primary Schools', Peshawar: BUNYAD.

British Council, 1999, Project Management Office, 'PTA Grants Survey: A Preliminary Analysis of Results for Donor Stakeholders', Islamabad.

Di Gropella, E., 1999, 'Education Decentralization Models in Latin America', *Cepal Review*, Vol. 68, pp. 156-73.

Elahi, M. Z., 1999, 'Establishing Partnerships', presented in the Sindh Primary Education Development, Government of Sindh/British Council Conference on Enhancing Capabilities for Community Participation—Revisiting Practices in Education Development, Karachi.

Eskeland, G. S., 2000, 'Autonomy, Participation and Learning in Argentina Schools: Findings and Implications for Decentralization?' World Bank, Washington DC.

Government of Punjab/MSU, 1998, 'Survey of School Management Committees in Districts D. G. Khan and Gujranwala', Department of Education, Islamabad.

Grootaert, C., G. Oh, and A. Swamy, 2002, 'Social Capital, Education, and Credit Markets: Empirical Evidence from Burkino Faso', in eds. Isham, J., T. Kelly, and S. Ramaswamy, *Social Capital and Economic Development: Well-Being in Developing Countries* (Cheltenham, UK: Edward Elgar).

Hussein, M. H., 1999, 'Decentralisation and Stakeholder Involvement in the Education Sector in Pakistan, A Review of Selected Strategies in the Education Sector: The School Management Committees and Collaboration with NGOs', Enterprise and Development Consultants, Islamabad.

The Institute for Educational Development, Aga Khan University, The University of Bristol and Oslo College, 1998, 'Some Lessons from Experience: A Report of a Joint Research Programme for the Norwegian Agency for Development Cooperation', Karachi.

Jimenez, E. and Y. Sawada, 1998, 'Do Community Managed Schools Work? An Evaluation of El Salvador's EDUCO Program', Working Paper Series on Impact Evaluation of Education Reforms Paper No. 8, Development Research Group, World Bank, Washington DC.

Khan, G. and M. A. Haque, 1999, 'Education for Development: The Causes, Consequences and Interactions of Human Capabilities', presented in the Sindh Primary Education Development, Government of Sindh/British Council Conference on Enhancing Capabilities for Community Participation—Revisiting Practices in Education Development, Karachi.

Khan, S. R. and F. Zafar, 1999, 'Capacity Building and Training of School Management Committees', SDPI Monograph Series No. 10.

Khan, S. R., 1999, *Government, Communities and NGOs in Social Sector Delivery: Collective Action in the Rural Water Supply Sector in Pakistan* (London: Ashgate).

Khan, S. R., 2001, 'Promoting Democratic Governance: The Case of Pakistan', *European Journal of Development Research*, Vol. 13, No. 2.

Khan, S. R., 2003, 'Participation and Collective Action in Government and NGO Schools', *Development in Practice*, Volume 13, No. 4.

King, E. M. and B. Özler, 'What's Decentralization Got to Do With Learning? The Case of Nicaragua's School Autonomy Reform', Development Research Group, World Bank, Washington DC.

King, E. M. and P. F. Orazem, 1999, 'Evaluating Education Reforms: Four Cases in Developing Countries', *The World Bank Economic Review*, Vol. 13, No. 3.

Khwendor Kor, 1999, (Nasreen Herald), PTA Project, 'Quarterly Progress Report for the Period March 1999-May 1999', Peshawar.

Merchant, N., 1999, 'Community Participation and Institutional Strengthening', presented in the Sindh Primary Education Development, Government of Sindh/British Council Conference on Enhancing Capabilities for Community Participation – Revisiting Practices in Education Development, Karachi.

Multi-Donor Support Unit (MSU), n.d., 'Seminar on Community Participation in School Education', 16 December 1998, Lahore.

Olson, M. (1971) *The Logic of Collective Action* (Cambridge, Massachusetts: Harvard University Press).

Eds. Randall, L., J. B. Anderson, 1999, *Schooling for Success: Preventing Repetition and Dropout in Latin American Primary Schools* (New York: M. E. Sharpe).

Social Action Programme Northern Areas, 1999, 'Operational Plan 1999-2000, SAP Coordination Unit', Gilgit, Northern Areas.

The World Bank, 1996, 'Improving Basic Education in Pakistan: Community Participation, System Accountability, and Efficiency', Islamabad.

Winkler, D. R. and A. I. Gershberg, 2000, 'Education Decentralization in Latin America: The Effects on the Quality of Schooling', World Bank Human.

Development Department, LCSHD Paper Series No. 59, Washington DC.

NOTES

1. This chapter draws on Khan (2003) and an earlier report written by Khan and Zafar (1999).
2. Only four private schools in our sample had formed an SMC or PTA.
3. For references to the literature on collective action and its application to rural water supply, see Khan (1999). Community is loosely defined here to mean the village (thus village and community are used interchangeably). Homogeneity neither exists nor is it implied. Participation and collective action is defined as all or a section of the villagers working collectively to deliver a service to themselves. This process could include voluntarism via a contribution in cash, kind, or labor.
4. Serving on PTAs is not generally compensated although it represents a real-time cost.
5. For a discussion of education in the devolution context in Pakistan, refer to Khan (2001).
6. This section is based on a much more detailed report on this subject written with Dr Fareeha Zafar. Refer to Khan and Zafar (1999).

7. The Development Research Group of the World Bank engaged in an attempt to distill lessons of decentralized education and the interested reader could get information on this and other citations from the World Bank website at http://www.worldbank.org.

8. Husein (1999, p. 8) argues that the real problems in education are the lack of accountability, lack of discipline, poor working conditions, poor incentives, and political interference and that SMCs/PTAs address none of these issues. In fact SMCs/PTAs are expected to address the first three issues and, if they were truly empowered, they would also have some say on the last two.

9. When the head teacher was to be replaced by a parent as the president of the SMC, the teacher unions went to court. The government viewed the notification as legal, but the unions took the plea that since the money was to be given to the SMCs, and that since they were most likely to misuse it, the teachers would be penalized as government servants. Since there was no ordinance or law pertaining to the legality of SMCs, in early September 1999, the government issued an ordinance giving legal cover to the SMCs. Thus the case filed by the unions was invalidated. The coming to power of the military government on 12 October 1999, and its focus on the devolution of powers to the grassroots level overshadowed this controversy.

10. In one case, the teachers put fans delivered via the SMC to personal use.

11. Also refer to the examples of SMCs in chapter 2.

12. For more details, refer to chapter 2, Annex 2.2, Case 5.

13. Henceforth, SMC is used to represent PTA unless we need to make a distinction. Since only four private schools in the sample had an SMC, we ignored these since this represents a very small number of observations for quantitative analysis. Also, while many more government and NGO schools had SMCs, the numbers in absolute terms are still small and, therefore, numbers are reported in parentheses whenever percentages are used.

4

The World Bank and Education

4.1. Introduction

The World Bank is one of the favorite targets for thinkers and writers on development issues. This is not surprising, since it is among the most influential actors in development. Its influence results from its direct and indirect control over development resources and from its enormous body of in-house and contracted research and publications on development issues.[1] The Bank is a moving target. Its openness to criticism and its willingness to absorb or co-opt ideas of critics seem to be more than just a public relations exercise. However, there is still a hard core of market oriented economic philosophy that critics contend is driven more by ideology than evidence. The education sector in Pakistan provides an interesting case study of the Bank's flexibility and willingness to absorb new ideas and for appraising and testing its maintained hypotheses.

The expression 'maintained hypotheses', as used here, requires some explanation. For example, estimating rates of returns, which became a growth industry in the economics of education literature, is drawn from human capital theory. While no authorship is being attributed to the World Bank for this, however, the Bank literature clearly maintains that this theory is valid and has actively promoted policy based on the estimation of rates of return.

Thus the Bank's influence in the education sector in Pakistan includes the promotion of Bank research showing a much higher social rate of return to primary education (classes 0-5) which coincided with the restructuring of expenditure within the education sector towards primary education.[2] Primary education expenditure during the Sixth Five Year Plan was 23.6 per cent of the total educational expenditure and this increased to an allocation of 47.5 per cent of the total for the Eighth Five Year Plan. Allocations at all other levels, except for teacher training, declined with expenditure at the college/university level declining from 19.5 per cent of the total to an allocation of 10.7 per cent.[3] Having been instrumental in the restructuring of educational expenditure to the primary level, the Bank was well placed for an exclusive focus on basic education (classes 0-8) as part of the Social Action Program (SAP) that was implemented in rural Pakistan in the 1990s and then discontinued due to suspected financial irregularities (see chapter 1).

Since the Bank is such a major player in development, the objective of this chapter is to conceptually and empirically examine the Bank's maintained hypotheses that pertain to basic education. In the second section, we discuss conceptual issues and identify hypotheses for testing. In the third section, we describe our method and present the results of testing hypotheses identified in the second section using schools as a unit of analysis, and we end with a summary.

4.2. Conceptual issues and testable hypotheses[4]

The implied recommendation of the proposition that the social rate of return to the primary level of education are the highest is a restructuring of educational expenditure towards primary and away from higher education, as indicated in the introduction. One can question the wisdom of educational expenditure restructuring based on social rates of return to education.[5] Implicit in the notion of rates of return to education is the acceptance of the decomposition of education into separate levels. While this may be necessary administratively, expenditure decisions need to be made in a manner that takes into account the linkages between different levels. More expenditure at the primary level requires expenditures on secondary and teacher education to produce more good quality teachers. Thus improving the state of primary schooling is not possible without also simultaneously improving secondary and teacher education, which in turn requires improving the quality of higher education.[6]

The allocation decisions based on rates of returns have also been challenged on a more fundamental level. The human capital theory underlying rates of return analysis is that, at all levels, education leads to higher productivity compared to the earlier level and the higher productivity is rewarded by higher pay on the job market. Scholars have questioned both these linkages on various grounds.[7] However, even if one were to accept the assumptions underlying human capital theory, basing current reallocation decisions that pertain to the future of current generations on the current aggregate experience of individuals on the job market would still be questionable.

An essential ingredient for computing rates of return to education, based on household survey data, is the construction of average age-earning profiles of individuals in the sample for each level of education. The difference between a higher and a lower level over time is assumed to constitute the average benefits from the higher level of education. However, there is no guarantee that the current earning profile will necessarily be reflective of the future. This is particularly the case when there is job upgradation with the spread of education so that employers start demanding higher academic qualifications for less skill or knowledge-intensive positions. In such a situation, a snapshot of the current age-earning profile can be quite misleading about the future education-earning scenario.[8]

If one assumes that individuals are rational, a fundamental postulate of human capital theory, then individuals should start reacting to market signals and start seeing the primary level merely as a stepping stone to higher levels of education. Thus, looking to the future, much of the value of primary level education, from the point of view of parents making the investment, is that it is a stepping-stone for higher levels of education. If that is the case, the presumption that one can sensibly decompose levels of education and separately calculate rates of returns to different levels of education once again comes into question.

Given these and other problems with rates of return analysis, one would have to make a justification for focusing on elementary education on other grounds. If fact, one can make strong arguments for such investments on both equity and efficiency grounds. Without being assured a start by the state via quality education, individuals below the poverty line may be completely denied any hope of realizing their intellectual potential and any hope for social mobility.[9] By providing an initial opportunity for intellectual growth at the widest level, such investment is equitable since it can reach a large number of those who would otherwise be deprived and it is efficient because by thus casting the net widely, in theory, the potential of the largest number can be tapped. Thus, due to equity and efficiency considerations, the state should ensure a basic education for all those not catered to by the non-government sector.

There is a large volume of World Bank literature on education. Since there is consistency in the viewpoint expressed in reports written for various countries, we have concentrated on Education Sector Strategy (1999) and reports written in the Pakistani context to identify important additional observations and hypotheses.[10] Among the observations are that government schools are so weak that it would be sensible to consider subsidies for the private sector and NGO schools (World Bank 1996, p. 12 and 1997, p. 12). Private sector schools are found to have lower unit costs due to lower teacher pay but better attendance and student performance. Similarly, subsidies are recommended for private teacher training colleges (1996, p. 37).

The reasoning for such subsidies may not be altogether sound on either market failure or equity grounds. The flat rate per student subsidy recommended for the better performing private sector schools is probably premised on the positive externalities expected to result from education. The existence of such externalities has been questioned, and even if they exist, they do not justify subsidizing a private sector activity.[11] There is little moral justification for the rest of society subsidizing a 'for-profit' activity. Alternative ways of encouraging schooling, including via the non-profit sector, can be found. Second, such a policy would create a moral hazard problem. Schools would be tempted to inflate reported enrollments to justify higher subsidies. Third, such subsidies do not discriminate between the poorest and the relatively more prosperous families. In fact, as pointed out in chapter 1, evidence shows that the poor are systematically excluded from schooling. It may therefore be more sensible to target the subsidies to the poorest families.[12]

There are various other hypotheses maintained in the World Bank literature on education that are not as provocative but nonetheless important to test. These include the hypotheses that in-service training is preferable to pre-service training; that relaxing teacher qualifications, raising class size, and multi-grade and multi-shift teaching would not hurt the acquisition of cognitive skills; and that user fees do not result in dropouts.[13] The commonality in all these hypotheses is that they generate cost saving, a major concern of World Bank led structural adjustment.[14]

4.3. Method, hypothesis testing and results

Our approach to testing the various hypotheses identified in section 4.2 is to use a crude production function approach with mean class 5 student cognitive skills (performance on math and comprehension tests) as the output and various mean teacher and school characteristics as inputs. Thus the unit of analysis is the school with the total sample size of 129 schools.

Sabot and Wakeman-Linn (1990) argue that production theory provides a reasonable theoretical underpinning for the statistical models estimating the determinants of performance.[15] At best, this holds true in a very crude input-output sense. In this approximate sense, teacher quality, teaching resources, student ability, student traits, and socio-economic status could be viewed as the inputs and student performance as the output.[16]

The basic production function estimated was as follows:

Performance = P (ST, SC, TQ, TT, OTC, SF)

Where
- ST = School type (government, private or NGO).
- SC = School characteristic (single-grade teaching, single-shift operation).
- TQ = Teacher qualifications [matriculate (class 10), higher secondary, bachelors and masters].
- TT = Teacher training. This includes pre-service training [primary teacher certificate (matriculation equivalent), certificate of teaching (higher secondary equivalent), higher qualifications (bachelors and masters equivalent] and in-service training.
- OTC = Other teacher characteristics (experience and teacher performance on math and comprehension tests).
- SF = Index of school facilities [School facilities is a composite index that in principle could range from 0 to 23 (actual mean and standard deviation are 14.6 and 3.9 respectively)] depending on access to facilities like lighting, desks, chairs, textbooks, notebooks, water, electricity, fans, washrooms, boards, chalk, charts, maps, models and library, etc.).

We first estimated the basic production function identified in equation 1 (results not reported).[17] The most significant findings from the estimates of both the math and comprehension production functions are that NGO and private schools produce much better results both statistically and quantitatively. NGO schools scored 1.54 and 7.55 points higher than government schools in math and comprehension tests which are 35 per cent and 56 per cent of the respective overall mean scores. Private schools scored 1.10 and 4.67 points higher than government schools in math and comprehension tests which are 25 per cent and 35 per cent of the respective overall mean scores.

By including interaction terms for NGO and private schools, we were able to decompose the variables that made a difference. The full set of interaction terms also helped us avoid having to estimate separate production functions by school type, which was not viable given that we have 129 observations in all. We also estimated an extended regression model with other relevant variables such as whether it was a single-gender school, students were provided help after hours, teachers provided private tuition (and consequently taught less in class), being a teacher was the first profession of choice, curricula was selected by the school, regular inspections, and teacher absentee rates. While most of these variables were not significant, including them in the model proved valuable since it demonstrated that the regression parameters of the 'core' statistical model were stable. Annex 4.1, Table 1 presents the results of the extended production function with interaction terms.

The maximum scores for the math and comprehension tests were 10 and 25 respectively and the means and standard deviations in our sample were 4.4 and 13.5 and 1.7 and 5.0 respectively. In both cases, the distributions were smooth and bell-shaped. The means are used as a benchmark for the interpretation of the parameters. For comprehension, class 5 performance in the private schools was significantly and substantially better than in government schools (i.e. 6.31 points higher). NGO or private sector performance in math was not significantly different from that in government schools.

Single-grade teaching did not significantly affect performance but performance in single-shift schools was better. Performance was 22 per cent better than the mean on comprehension tests and 54 per cent better on math tests. Higher teacher qualifications did not accompany better student performance with the exception of a negative effect at the masters' level for comprehension tests. Here, the problem may be public sector teachers with a masters' degree. The mean comprehension score of students who had NGO and private sector teachers with a masters' degree is 4.3 and 8.5 points higher than for students of a class teacher with a masters' degree in the public sector.

Teacher experience is positive and significant, but enhances scores in comprehension and math by just over 2 per cent. Higher teacher scores in math enhance student scores in math by 5.4 per cent. Higher level teacher training qualifications leads to 17 per cent improvement in math scores and a 20 per cent improvement in comprehension scores while in-service training added 14 per cent to math scores but had no impact on comprehension scores.

School facilities have a negative and significant sign, but NGOs and the private sector with better school facilities had students performing about a quarter point higher than in government schools. As maintained by Bank documents, higher student-teacher ratios did not adversely affect performance.

We did not have enough observations to rigorously test the proposition that user charges do not impact school attendance since we were only able to track seventeen students who dropped out during the school year. However, 35 per cent of these seventeen students (the largest among the various categories) mentioned they had dropped out because they could not afford the schooling. This finding confirms the results of a national survey of 16,182 households conducted by the Federal Bureau of Statistics in 2001–2002, reported on in chapter 1. Once again, schooling being 'too expensive' was the largest among the various categories of responses and about 29 per cent and 40 per cent of the students respectively dropped out or never attended school for this reason.[18]

Among the variables included in the extended model, teachers who provided extra help to students in NGO schools produced a 13 per cent better performance in comprehension. An interesting policy lesson seemed to emerge from the much better math performance (27 per cent higher) in NGO primary schools and primary units in middle schools relative to primary units in high schools. However, this finding is negated by poorer performance in comprehension in the NGO middle school primary sections relative to the high school primary section. More empirical support is needed on this and the other findings reported above. In the next chapter, we use students rather than class as the unit of analysis and cover some of the same ground as in this chapter.

Summary

Based on the presumption that the human-capital-theory-based rates of returns to education are a sound tool for the allocation of resources in the education sector, the World Bank was instrumental in a massive reallocation towards primary education and away from higher education. However, while rates of returns may be a valuable tool for inter-sectoral allocations, it has several flaws making them suspect as a sensible tool for intra-sectoral allocations. Again, based on evidence that private and NGO sector schools are much more cost-effective than government schools, World Bank literature has advocated subsidies for the non-government sector which can be challenged on several counts. Apart from discussing conceptual reservations with World Bank maintained hypotheses, we also tested several other hypotheses, most of which seem to be driven by a cost-saving objective.

There is support for the view that NGO and private schools are more efficient in delivering education. We also found support for several of the other World Bank maintained hypotheses that push for economies. Contrary to our prior expectations, higher student-teacher ratios did not negatively impact math and comprehension test scores, single-grade teaching did not improve them, and higher teacher qualifications did not have a positive impact on test scores. However, contrary to what the World Bank maintains, single-shift schools and higher pre-service teacher training did have a significant and sizable positive impact on test scores. Our main concern in this research is with questioning 'certainties' rather than with establishing them. Given the small size of our data set, we view our results as suggestive.

References

Behrman, J. R., 1990, 'Human Resource Externalities on a Micro Level in Rural Pakistan', draft prepared for the Pakistan Rural Education Research Team funded from a US AID grant.

Carnoy, M., 1995, 'Structural Adjustment and the Changing Face of Education', *International Labour Review*, Vol. 134, No. 6, pp. 653-73.

Fine, B. and P. Rose, 2001, 'Education and the Post-Washington Consensus', in eds. B. Fine, C. Lapavistsas, and J. Pincus, *Development Policy in the Twenty-first Century: Beyond the post-Washington Consensus* (London: Routledge).

Government of Pakistan, 2002, 'Pakistan Integrated Household Survey', Federal Bureau of Statistics, Islamabad.

Government of Pakistan, 1993, *Eighth Five Year Plan 1993-98*, Draft Report on Education and Training Sector, Annexure I, Planning Commission, Islamabad.

Government of Pakistan, 1988, *Seventh Five Year Plan 1988-93*, Planning Commission, Islamabad.

Kennedy, P., 2003, *A Guide to Econometrics* (5th. ed.) (Cambridge, Mass.: The MIT Press).

Khan, S. R., 1993, 'Underestimates of Aggregate Rates of Return to Education', *International Journal of Manpower*, Vol. 14, No. 8, pp. 17-22.

Psacharopoulos, G., 1994, 'Returns to Education: A Global Update', *World Development*, Vol. 22, No. 9, pp. 1325-43.

Sabot, R., and J. Wakeman-Linn, (1990), 'Determinants of Performance in Introductory Courses in Economics and Seven Other Disciplines'. Williams College, draft.

Schultz, T. P., 1988, 'Education Investments and Returns', in eds. H. Chenery and T. N. Srinivasan, Handbook of Development Economics, Vol. 1 (New York: Elsevier Science Publishers).

Eds. Van de Walle, D. and K. Nead, 1995, *Public Spending and the Poor* (Baltimore: Johns Hopkins).

World Bank, 1996, 'Improving Basic Education in Pakistan: Community Participation, System Accountability, and Efficiency', Population and Human Resource Development Division, South Asia Region, Washington DC.

World Bank, 1997, 'Towards a Strategy for Elementary Education', Population and Human Resource Development Division, South Asia Region, Washington DC.

World Bank, 1999, 'Education: Education Sector Strategy', Washington DC.

Annex 4.1

Table 1:   Determinants of class 5 comprehension and math performance

Predictors/Dependent variables	Comprehension	Maths
Constant	5.023***	-0.169
	(1.718)	(0.181)
School Type and Characteristics		
NGO	3.458	1.196
	(0.728)	(0.069)
Private	6.316*	- 0.149
	(3.997)	(0.074)
Single-grade teaching (SG)	-0.077	- 0.321
	(0.088)	(1.092)
Single-shift school (SS)	3.016*	2.387*
	(3.227)	(6.877)
NGO * SS	- 5.870*	- 1.972**
	(3.354)	(2.318)
NGO*Primary school	-	1.173**
		(2.382)
NGO*Middle school	-2.477**	1.195**
	(1.973)	(2.169)
Teacher Qualification		
Higher secondary	0.038	0.190
	(0.266)	(0.486)
Bachelors	-0.666	0.395
	(0.454)	(0.880)
Masters (MA)	- 5.288**	0.289
	(2.219)	(0.584)
NGO * MA	4.341**	-
	(2.063)	
Private * MA	8.538*	-
	(2.910)	
Teacher Training		
Certificate teaching (CT)	- 0.901	0.207
	(1.042)	(0.564)
Private * CT	-	- 2.050*
		(2.248)
Higher teaching certificates	2.640**	0.757***
	(2.302)	(1.782)
In-service training (IST)	0.389	0.615**
	(0.469)	(1.974)

NGO * IST		- 1.228* (2.535)
Other Teacher Characteristics		
Experience (Exp)	0.299** (2.400)	0.099* (3.165)
NGO * Exp	-0.301*** (2.024)	-
Private * Exp	- 0.295** (2.332)	- 0.101* (3.005)
Teacher performance (TP) in comprehension/math	0.004 (0.055)	0.239* (5.375)
NGO * TP	0.493* (2.856)	-
Private * TP	-	- 0.180** (1.987)
Other schooling characteristics		
Student-teacher ratio	0.033 (0.877)	0.013 (1.053)
NGO*Extra help for students	1.776*** (1.685)	-
School Facilities (SF)	- 0.101 (0.708)	- 0.114** (2.330)
NGO * SF	-	0.152*** (1.722)
Private * SF	-	0.256*** (1.856)
R bar Sq.	0.32	0.31
F-Stat.	3.73*	3.51*
N	129	129

Notes: *   = Significant at least at the 1 per cent level
      **   = Significant at least at the 5 per cent level
      *** = Significant at least at the 10 per cent level

The Brecusch – Pagan test was used to test for heteroscedasticity, and the results are corrected for it. The base categories are government for school type, matric (class 10) for teacher qualifications, and primary teacher certificate for teacher training certification. All other variables are binary, with one representing the presence of a characteristic, except for teacher experience, teacher performance and school facilities, which are continuous.

NOTES

1. The direct control over resources is its annual lending program and the indirect control is the considerable influence it exercises on other multi-lateral and bi-lateral aid agencies. This also applies to the IMF, the Bank's sister organization. The Fund is much more uncompromising in its economic philosophy. Notwithstanding some probably sincere statements about a concern for poverty made by senior Fund officials, there is much less dust clouding what the Fund stands for.

2. Psacharopoulos (1994) at the World Bank compiled the relevant evidence based on Bank research and other studies.

3. Seventh Five Year Plan 1988-98, (1988, p. 417), Eighth Five Year Plan 1993-98, Draft Report on Education and Training Sector, Annexure I.

4. Refer to Fine and Rose (2001) for a critique of World Bank policy on education.

5. For an extensive review of other methodological critiques refer to Schultz (1988).

6. In its Education Sector Strategy (1999, p. 24), the Bank states that the 'staff now look at education as an integrated system, one part of which cannot function well if another is ailing'. This is a welcome change in view, even if late in coming.

7. Gender barriers and discrimination would in particular sever such links. Khan (1993, pp. 17-18) cites references to the relevant literature, including to alternative explanations of why the links posited to exist by human capital theory may not hold.

8. The computation of social rates of return to education, as opposed to the private rates of return, requires making several adjustments to arrive at estimates that more closely measure the contribution of a certain amount of schooling to society after accounting for market failures. However, the problems that we identify here carry over to the measurement of the social rate of return.

9. In chapter 1, section 1.4.2., we show that many poor children either do not attend school or drop out if they do attend.

10. The World Bank website mentioned that the World Bank Strategy paper would be updated in 2004, but this had not been done by the time this chapter was revised (October, 2004). Reports in the Pakistani context include World Bank (1996) and World Bank (1997).

11. Behrman, J. R., (1990).

12. Eds. van de Walle and Nead (1995), in particular the paper by A. K. Sen.

13. The World Bank (1997) report on education in Pakistan asserts that good primary education is possible with thirty-five to forty students per teacher.

14. A useful source on the Bank's maintained hypotheses in a structural adjustment context is Carnoy (1995).

15. For a more detailed discussion of the method and qualifications refer to chapter 5.

16. Performance is also likely to depend on non-observable student traits and innate ability. We assume a normal distribution of these traits and innate ability within the class.

17. Grouping leads to a loss in efficiency because of a loss of information in the aggregation process. However, this is not necessarily the case and aggregation can cancel out errors of measurement. Heteroscedasticity is a problem and that has been corrected for. Refer to Kennedy (2003, p. 544).

18. Government of Pakistan (2002, pp. 47-8).

5

Educational Production Functions:
A Quantitive Analysis

5.1. Introduction

Chapter 4 is quantitative analysis using classes as the unit of analysis, while this chapter also estimates education production functions, students are the unit of analysis. However, as indicated in chapter 4, there is controversy in the literature about whether production theory provides a reasonable theoretical underpinning for the statistical models estimating the determinants of student performance. Very roughly, the econometrics entails having some measure of student performance on the left hand side (output) and various measures of 'inputs' explaining student performance on the right hand side. These include school, family, teacher, and community variables. From a policy perspective, the purpose of such estimation is to identify the key inputs that would enhance student performance.

This technique has been in use for a long time, and Hanushek (1986) has provided a useful survey of the earlier literature. Skepticism of the value of this tool has not abated over time, and Hodas (1993) is an example of why some scholars see little value in the use of educational production functions. Based on the earlier literature, the argument is that educational production functions are too aggregate and are unable to capture the complex process in the classroom that explains student performance. Similarly, Hanushek and Haribison (1989, p. 9) point out that qualitative differences in teacher behavior are difficult to model statistically.

Thus, the upshot is that unobservable or unmeasured influences, missing from the right hand side and systematically associated with included variables, would limit the value of the remaining coefficients in the specification. While these are powerful arguments, policy makers nonetheless need some advice on what are likely to be the most effective ways of expending resources. Thus, abandoning this research program may be too extreme a response to the limitations of empirical modeling.

Another line of criticism, as is the case with Fortune (1993) or Monk (1992), is to accept the basic value of the tool, but to point out the various statistical flaws in its use and suggest improvements. Goldhaber and Brewer (1997, pp. 506-7) summarize some of the major statistical shortcomings of the production function estimates. These include the impact of unobservable factors, the lack of measures on test scores that can net out the impact of innate individual ability, and the lack of panel data enabling the tracking of students to measure value added or progress over time as the appropriate left hand side variable.[2] Figlio (1998) questions the restrictive functional forms generally used in educational production function studies.[3] Apart from these fundamental shortcomings, there are a host of measurement problems that could arise resulting from aggregation, omitted variable bias, and the use of crude proxy variables.

Cooper and Cohn (1997) mention the different possible measures of output of the education process. In a broad sense, this could be the contribution to individuals becoming good citizens. In a more narrow sense, this could represent success on the labor market and a contribution to higher earnings, the completion of formal education, or simply graduation to the next level. Most education production studies now use performance on standardized tests as a measure of output.

Of particular relevance to the topic of this chapter is the research on school choice. Hoxby (1994), Goldhaber (1996) and Figlio and Stone (1999) have contributed to this debate. Also relevant is Levin (1997) who applies the concept of X-inefficiency to raising school productivity. Thus he argues that better organization, information flows, and incentives could raise school performance. Our focus on intangibles and school morale complements this approach.

While the debate continues, scholars have addressed the various critiques with better data and more refined statistical methods.[4] This chapter seeks to contribute to the literature from an institutional perspective in several ways, while addressing key policy issues pertaining to basic education in rural Pakistan. First, in keeping with the main themes of this book, we explore performance by type of ownership. In Pakistan, not unlike many other developing countries, the three main categories of schools are government, private and NGO (non-government or non-profit organization). Not accounting for the institutional difference could also bias the estimates. Thus, our production function estimation is cast in a comparative institutional context. Second, following from chapter 4, there are various economies proposed regarding primary schooling and we test the performance impact of instituting these economies. These include the hypotheses that in-service training is preferable to pre-service training; that relaxing teacher qualifications, raising class size, and multi-grade and multi-shift teaching would not hurt the acquisition of cognitive skills. The commonality in all these hypotheses, as indicated in chapter 4, is that they generate cost saving, a major concern of World Bank led education sector reform.[5] Third, following the earlier literature, we investigate if particular school policies and inputs are more likely than others to contribute to better student performance in a developing country context. Finally, we had a highly qualified field team observe schools and rate them based on features or 'intangibles' that are missed by quantitative data sets because they are difficult to measure.

In the sections that follow, the conceptual approach utilized for the estimation is presented in section 2 and the findings are presented in section 3. We end with a summary.

5.2. Conceptual and statistical approach

Educational production functions common in the literature are used for exploring the various research questions identified in the introduction. Cognitive skills (performance on math and comprehension tests) for class 5 students are used as the output and various teacher (TC), student (SC), family (FC), and school characteristics as the inputs. Thus, the unit of analysis is individual students. School characteristics have been divided into policy (SP) and facility variables (SF). To the generally used inputs, we have also added the school evaluation by the field team for the determination of the importance of 'intangibles'.

As explained in the introduction, many scholars view production theory as a reasonable theoretical underpinning for the statistical models estimating the determinants of performance. We anticipated selectivity in the production of cognitive skills depending on which type of school the parents opted for, and so the math and comprehension production functions are corrected for sample selection.[6] The production function estimated after selection control was as follows:

Performance = P (FC,SC,TC,SP,SF, SE)
Where

FC	=	Family characteristics. These include parent's education and whether they check the child's homework.[7]
SC	=	Student characteristics. This includes the student absentee record.[8]
TC	=	Teacher characteristics. These include qualifications [matriculate (class 10), higher secondary, bachelors and masters], teacher training [primary teacher certificate (matriculation or tenth grade equivalent)], certificate of teaching (higher secondary equivalent), higher qualifications (bachelors and masters equivalent) and in-service training). Other teacher characteristics include experience and teacher performance on math and comprehension tests, and their absentee rate.
SP	=	School policy. These include student-teacher ratio, type of school (mixed, all-boy or all-girl, independent primary school or part of middle or high school), teaching policy (single-grade teaching, single-shift teaching), homework policy, language policy (teaching in mother tongue), curriculum policy (selecting own curriculum), inspection policy, absentee policy (imposing fines etc.), testing policy (weekly, monthly, term, or annual), parental participation policy (shown homework and report cards) and corporal punishment policy.
SF	=	School facilities. These include access to facilities like desks, chairs (for teachers and students), water, electricity, washrooms, chalk, charts, models and libraries.
SE	=	School evaluation by the field team of the school as successful, unsuccessful, or mixed.

5.3. Findings[9]

The field team subjective evaluations in Table 2.1. are contrasted in Table 5.1 below with the average test scores attained by students by school type included in the sample for the quantitative analysis.

Table 5.1 Average math and comprehension scores for sample students of government, private, and NGO schools

Subjects/school type	Math	Comprehension	n
Government	4.30 (2.18)	10.68 (6.20)	750
Private	4.68 (2.37)	14.00 (6.23)	608
NGO	5.01 (1.77)	16.60 (5.43)	693

Source: SDPI Survey.

Notes: Parentheses include standard deviations and n represents the numbers of students who took the test. The maximum possible score for the math and comprehension tests respectively were 10 and 25 respectively. The F-statistics were 20.41 and 179.12 respectively representing a significant difference across school type. Column 4 provides the sub-sample size (n).

The findings in Table 5.1 above regarding mean scores on math and comprehension tests by school type are consistent with the subjective evaluations of the different types of schools. NGO schools reveal the best performance followed by private schools with the government schools showing the poorest performance.

The means and standard deviations of the variables used in the estimation are reported in Annex 5.1, Table 1. There are some notable differences across the three types of institutions, although these are not surprising. Government teachers are more experienced, more educated, and have more training invested in them than private or NGO sector teachers. However, they also had a higher absentee rate than private and NGO sector teachers. Students going to private and NGO schools came from much wealthier backgrounds and their parents were much more educated. Thus, not surprisingly, children in private and NGO schools were more likely than children in government schools to show their report cards to their parents and a higher percentage of such parents were likely to sign the report cards. As shown to be nationally true in chapter 1, facilities in private and NGO schools were far better than those in government schools.

The results of the probit demand for school type equation estimated to control for selection are reported in Annex 5.1, Table 2a. Lambda (the Inverse Mills ratio) is highly significant in all the comprehension equations suggesting that selection was an issue. In the math equations, lambda was not significant and so the production functions were estimated using ordinary least squares. The production function estimates are reported in Annex 5.1, Table 2b and Table 3.[10]

Some interesting findings emerged from the probit selection estimation.[11] Boys were more likely than girls to attend a government school and girls more likely to attend an NGO school. The greater the number of school-going siblings in the household made it less likely for a child to attend a private school. Older children were less likely to attend an NGO school. Finally, and most important, attending a government school was inversely associated with income group. All income groups were more likely to attend government schools than the rich. However, the poor and extremely poor were less likely than the rich to attend private and NGO schools.

Higher school fees are more likely to identify households attending private and NGO schools.[12] Thus, as expected, school fee varies inversely for selection into government schools and positively with NGO and private schools. The interaction terms of fee and income group reinforce this finding and children of all income groups, compared to the richer families, were more likely to be associated with government schools due to the higher fee.

Comprehension and math tests for students were developed using the syllabi of various textbook boards developed for class 5. The dependent variables were scores on math and comprehension tests and the maximum scores were 10 and 25 respectively.[13]

Among family variables, mother's education had a positive and significant impact on math scores for private schools and on comprehension scores for both government and private schools.[14] Father's education was positive and significant only for NGO schools for both subjects and in government schools for math scores. The number of educated siblings in the family had a positive impact on both comprehension and math scores of students going to private schools. Among the student characteristics, age had a positive and significant impact in the case of government schools and girls scored significantly less (1.3 points) in the comprehension test in private schools.

Many of the teacher characteristics proved to be important. Teacher's math and comprehension scores had a significant positive impact on student math and comprehension scores in NGO schools. Teacher's qualifications reveal an interesting story. In government schools, higher qualifications actually took away from the teacher's ability to produce better student results. Relative to a teacher with a matriculate degree (10 grades), teachers who had an intermediate degree (12 grades) were associated with 8.4 points lower student scores, and those who had a masters degree (12 per cent of total teachers) were associated with a 5.6 points lower student score respectively in comprehension tests. Similarly, math scores were respectively 1.2 and 1.6 points lower. Given the automatic tenure and the higher pay for higher qualifications, the more senior teachers were probably not motivated (refer to chapter 6 for more on teachers). The higher absentee rate among teachers in government schools is also suggestive of disinterest and a lack of discipline.

For private schools, this result was reversed. In private schools, relative to teachers with a matriculate degree, teachers with an intermediate, bachelors' and masters' degree were respectively associated with 2.2, 2.5 and 3.1 points higher student scores in math. Again, those who possessed an intermediate or masters' degree were associated with 5.1 and 6.4 points higher student scores respectively in private schools. These results are suggestive of a more effective utilization of resources in private schools that exercise their right to hire and fire at will.

More intensive teacher training showed mixed results. Thus relative to a primary teacher certificate (PTC) or those with no training, class teachers with a certificate of teaching (CT) in private schools were associated with 12 points and 2.8 points higher student score in the comprehension and math tests respectively. NGO school class teachers with CT were associated with a 0.9 points higher student math score. Class teachers who had earned the higher certificate of training (HCT), not common for NGO or private schools, were associated with 2.8 points higher math scores in government schools.

NGOs are reputed for their in-service training and this showed up in the comprehension test scores. Thus, teachers who had received in-service training in NGO schools were associated with 2.4 points higher test scores in student comprehension tests. The private sector may have been directing its in-service training towards the weaker teachers since they are associated with 4 points lower scores in student comprehension tests.

Teachers' experience had a positive and significant impact on student test scores in half the cases, although the magnitude was small. We inquired from the teachers if being a teacher was their first preference. A 'yes' response was associated with almost two points higher score on comprehension test scores of students in government schools and the reverse in private schools. However, it accounted for a 1 point higher score in student math scores in private schools.

Two teacher practices in government schools are widely viewed as having a negative impact on student performance. These include high teacher absentee rates and the practice of providing tuition after class. Many parents complain that since teachers make money by providing tuition after class, they do not have an incentive to teach in class. For the most part, neither practice had much impact on test scores. Math scores were 0.7 points higher in private schools for students of teachers providing tuition. It is possible that the more successful teachers managed to find students for tuition.

A number of the school policy characteristics were significant. Since over-crowding is not a problem in NGO and private schools, it is not surprising that a higher student–teacher ratio was actually associated with a positive and significant but negligibly higher student test scores for math. For government schools, higher student-teacher ratios were significantly and negatively associated with student test scores in both math and comprehension, but the magnitude was negligible.

Economies in education can also be sought from double-shift school policy or multi-grade teaching. Our results show that students in single-shift schools performed better than those in double-shift schools. Comprehension scores were respectively 6.3 and 7.1 points higher for students of government and private schools and math scores were 1.7 points higher for students of NGO schools. Surprisingly, students in multi-grade classes performed respectively 0.7 and 0.9 points higher in government and NGO schools.

Another policy variable is whether girls and boys should be encouraged to study in separate schools. Many parents in a conservative Muslim culture prefer this, but NGO and private schools generally run mixed classes at the primary level. Having separate schools made a difference for comprehension test scores in the all-girl government schools. These girls scored an average of 3.7 points higher in comprehension test scores (34 per cent of the mean) than girls in co-education government schools. However, the reverse was true for math scores that were 1.5 points lower (43 per cent of the mean) in the government all-girls schools than in the government co-education schools.

A policy of having students repeat a class if the performance is below par did not make a difference to student performance in the sense that, in no case, did they out-perform students that had not repeated. One of the reasons for government school performance being poorer than NGO and private schools could be a lack of accountability. Students in government and private schools that were regularly inspected scored 4.6 and 6.5 points lower on comprehension scores in the government and private schools respectively and 1.6 points lower on math for the private schools. Perhaps the causality is reversed and the poorer schools draw more inspection. For NGO schools, regular inspection was associated with about a one point higher test score in math.

Assigning homework regularly only makes a difference for government schools. Regular homework improves student comprehension test scores by 1.2 points and math test scores by 0.3 points respectively in government schools. Educationists in Pakistan have advocated teaching in the mother tongue at the primary level.[15] Our findings show that the results from pursuing such a policy are mixed. Such a policy does not appear to make a difference for government schools, but students being taught in their mother tongue scored respectively 5.7 and 1.5 points higher in comprehension and math tests in private schools, but respectively 4.5 and 2 points lower in NGO schools. Students in NGO schools that had flexibility in setting the curriculum scored 2.7 points higher in comprehension test scores.

A school policy of imposing fines to curb absenteeism did not generally help test scores to improve. Math scores in government and private schools with such a policy in place were respectively 1.0 and 0.9 points lower and comprehension scores in government schools were 8 points lower. However, in this case again, the causality may be reversed in that such a policy may only be imposed in schools with a chronic student absentee problem. In NGO schools, such a school policy was associated with 1.5 points higher scores in comprehension tests.

A policy of trying to get the parents involved in the child's schooling had limited success in improving test scores. Requiring parents to read the report card improved comprehension test scores only for private schools by 4.7 points and our results show that requiring the signing of report cards had no impact.

Alternatives to annual tests are often proposed as a mechanism to keep children focused to improve performance. We explored for the performance outcome of weekly, monthly and term (semester) tests relative to annual tests and the results were mixed. Weekly tests were associated with respectively 2 points and 1 point higher scores in comprehension and math tests in government schools but with 2.6 points lower comprehension scores in NGO school. Monthly tests were associated with about a 1 point lower math test score in private schools.

Independent primary schools, rather than those associated as units with middle (up to class 8) or higher schools (up to class 10) are expected to produce better performance. This is because primary students can be marginalized as much more importance is devoted to students at a higher level who sit for board exams and hence contribute to the school's reputation. The converse argument is that primary units that are a part of higher levels have access to more resources. Our findings show that students in independent primary schools scored 5.3 points higher in comprehension scores in government schools but 5.7 points lower in private schools. Independent primary schools were associated with respectively 1.9 and 0.9 points higher math scores for private and NGO schools. Similarly, primary units in middle schools were associated with 4.4 points higher comprehension scores in government schools and with respectively 0.8 and 1.9 points higher math scores in private and NGO schools.

The two other policy variables we explored concerned whether children in the schools were beaten and whether the schools provided extra help to the weaker students after school. The conventional wisdom of 'spare the rod and spoil the child' still prevails in rural schools in Pakistan. Our findings show little support for this policy that is still widespread.[16] Only students in private schools produced 0.3 points higher score in math tests. Providing extra help to the weaker students improved the average test scores more widely. Comprehension test scores were respectively 4.2 points and 7.2 points higher for students in government and private schools providing such help after school. However, math scores were 1.2 points lower with such a policy suggesting a causality issue once again.

School facilities provide no clear policy direction, perhaps due to multicollinearity.[17] Several of the coefficients had unexpected negative signs. We report results in the very few cases where a clear policy direction emerges. Holding class outdoors, because of inadequate indoor facilities, resulted in 3.3 points lower test scores in comprehension for government schools and 3 points lower test scores in math for NGO schools. Not having electricity resulted in 4.5 points lower test scores in comprehension for government schools.

The final variable of interest for us was the success of the field-team evaluation of the schools based on their observation of intangibles. Schools were rated as successful, mixed or unsuccessful based on these observations as indicated in chapter 2. Students in government and private schools evaluated as successful scored respectively 6.2 and 6.4 points higher in comprehension and 2.0 and 2.9 points higher in math scores than those ranked as unsuccessful. However, students in the 'unsuccessful' NGO schools scored 1.1 points higher in math than those ranked as successful.[18] Students of government and private schools evaluated as mixed scored respectively 7.6 and 2.0 points higher in comprehension scores and 3.6 points higher in math scores for government schools relative to the unsuccessful schools.

Summary

This chapter uses a production function approach to identify the impact of student, parent, teacher, and school characteristics on student test scores in math and comprehension. It also evaluates the importance of 'intangibles' and cost-cutting and other policy variables in a comparative institutional context. Many of the findings add to the body of empirical evidence so that empirical regularities, repeated often enough, become part of accepted knowledge regarding schooling in a developing-country context. Our findings based on the policy variables are interesting and, if replicated enough times, would become part of this body of knowledge.

Teacher math and comprehension scores were associated with higher student math and comprehension scores for NGO schools. The impact of teacher qualifications on student test scores varied by school type. In government schools, where teachers have tenure and salary contingent on qualifications and experience, qualifications were inversely associated with student cognitive skill scores. In private schools, in which there is no tenure policy and school management has the power to hire and fire at will, higher teacher qualifications were positively and significantly associated with higher student cognitive skills and the magnitudes involved were high. This unexpectedly emerged as one of our most important policy findings.

The importance of teacher training is sometimes disputed. Our results showed that in both government and private schools, higher levels of teacher training have a sizable impact on student achievement. In NGO schools, in-service training, which is what they are often reputed for, proved to be positively associated with comprehension test scores. Teacher experience had positive and significant coefficients in three of the six specifications, but the magnitude of the coefficients were small.

Among school characteristics, many policy variables only made a difference in government schools that are in any case our main policy focus. Crowding is much more likely in government schools, and student-teacher ratios were inversely associated with comprehension test scores in only government schools, but the impact was negligible. Average comprehension scores of girls studying in single-gender government schools were notably higher than for girls studying in co-education schools for comprehension, but the reverse was the case for math. This was not an issue in private or NGO schools. The policy of assigning regular homework made a difference only for government schools and single-shift teaching improved comprehension test scores in government schools. Remedial assistance for weak students after school was associated with higher comprehension test scores in government schools. Finally, there is likely to be a payoff from more regularly testing in government schools than relying on annual exams. There was little support for the policy of allowing corporal punishments to improve performance. In view of the negative psychological repercussions and the continued wide prevalence of this practice, corporal punishments for children should be banned.

Due to the large number of variables utilized as predictors, it was difficult to identify the precise significance of various school facilities. However, outdoor teaching and the lack of electricity were associated with poorer student test scores in government schools.

Finally, there is support for the view that intangibles do make a difference in schooling. For government and private schools, the field team evaluation of schools as successful or having mixed success resulted in significantly higher test scores for both subjects than for the schools the field team judged unsuccessful. These intangibles were evaluated by a highly educated field team, but nonetheless not by professional educationists. Thus, one can only view this finding as a beginning and there is scope for much more research on this issue.

References

Alderman, H., J. R. Behrman, S. R. Khan, D. R. Ross and R. Sabot, 1995, 'Public Schooling Expenditures in Rural Pakistan: Efficiently Targeting Girls and a Lagging Region', in eds. D. van de Walle and K. Nead, *Public Spending and the Poor: Theory and Evidence* (Baltimore: Johns Hopkins University Press).

Alderman, H., J. R. Behrman, D. R. Ross and R. H. Sabot, 1996, 'Decomposing the Gender Gap in Cognitive Skills in a Poor Rural Economy', *Journal of Human Resources*, Volume 31.

Carnoy, M., 1995, 'Structural Adjustment and the Changing Face of Education', *International Labour Review*, Vol. 134, No. 6.

Coates, D., 2003, 'Education Production Functions Using Instructional Time as an Input', *Education Economics*, Vol. 11, No. 3.

Cooper, S. T. and E. Cohn, 1997, 'The Estimation of a Frontier Production Function for the South Carolina Educational Process', *Economics of Education Review*, Vol. 16, No. 3.

Figlio, D. N. and J. A. Stone, 1999, 'Are Private Schools Really Better?', *Research in Labor Economics*, Vol. 18.

Figlio, D. N., 1998, 'Functional Form and the Estimated Effects of School Resources', *Economics of Education Review*, Vol. 18, No. 2.

Fortune, J. C., 1993, 'Why Production Function Analysis is Irrelevant in Policy Deliberations Concerning Education Funding Equity', *Education Policy Analysis Archives*, Vol. 1, No. 11.

Goldhaber, D. D., 1996, 'Public and Private High Schools: Is School Choice an Answer to the Productivity Problem', *Economics and Education Review*, Vol. 15, No. 2.

Goldhaber, D. D. and D. J. Brewer, 1997, 'Why Don't Schools and Teachers Seem to Matter?: Assessing the Impact of Unobservables on Education Production', *Journal of Human Resources*, Vol. 32, No. 3.

Hanushek, E.A., 1986, 'The Economics of Schooling: Production and Efficiency in Public School', *Journal of Economic Literature*, Vol. 24, No. 3.

Hanushek, E. A. and R. W. Harbison, 1989, 'Investments in School Quality: Evidence from Brazil', Paper prepared for a Conference on Family, Gender Differences, and Development, Yale University, September 4-6, draft.

Heckman, J., 1976, 'The Common Structure of Statistical Models of Truncation, Sample Selection and Limited Dependent Variables', *Annals of Economic and Social Measurement*, 5a.

Hodas, S., 1993, 'Is Water an Input to a Fish? Problems with the Production Function Model in Education', *Education Policy Analysis Archives*, Vol. 1, No. 12.

Hoxby, C. M., 1994, 'Do Private Schools Provide Competition for Public Schools?' National Bureau of Economic Research, Working Paper No. 4978.

Khan, M. A., 1993, 'Reports and Papers Prepared Under the Provisions of HRD Component of the Pakistan Project: Comments and Queries', Baltimore, The Johns Hopkins University, mimeo.

Knight, J. B. and R. H. Sabot, 1990, *Education, Productivity and Inequality: The East African Natural Experiment* (New York: Oxford University Press).

Krueger, A. B., 1999, 'Experimental Estimates of Education Production Functions', *Quarterly Journal of Economics*, Vol. 114, No. 2.

Levin, J., 2001, 'For Whom the Reductions Count: A Quintile Regression Analysis of Class Size and Peer Effects on Scholastic Achievement', *Empirical Economics*, Vol. 26, No. 1.

Levin, H. M., 1997, 'Raising School Productivity: An X-Efficiency Approach', *Economics of Education Review*, Vol. 16, No. 3.

Monk, D. H., 1992, 'Education Productivity Research: An Update and Assessment of its Role in Education Finance Reform', *Education Evaluation and Policy Analysis*, Vol. 14, No. 4.

Todd, P. E. and K. I. Wolpin, 2003, 'On the Specification and Estimation of Production Function for Cognitive Achievement', *The Economic Journal*, Vol. 113, No. 4.

Vignoles, A., R. Levacic, J. Walker, S. Machin and D. Reynolds, 2000, 'The Relationship Between Resource Allocation and Pupil Attainment', Centre for the Economics of Education, London School of Economics, London, draft.

Wilson, K., 2001, 'The Determinants of Educational Attainment: Modeling and Estimating the Human Capital Model and Education Production Functions', *Southern Economic Journal*, Vol. 67, No. 3.

Annex 5.1

Table 1: Mean and standard deviation of variables used in the production function estimations.

Variables	Government	Private	NGO
FAMILY CHARATERISTICS (FC)			
Father's education	5.54	7.84	7.91
	(4.69)	(5.01)	(4.84)
Mother's education	1.63	3.65	2.97
	(3.13)	(4.39)	(3.88)

Number of educated siblings	3.58	3.37	3.49
	(1.68)	(1.66)	(1.59)
Parents check homework	0.42	0.64	0.60
Extremely poor	0.13	0.05	0.05
Poor	0.53	0.28	0.30
Middle class	0.32	0.51	0.50
Rich	0.02	0.15	0.14
STUDENT CHARACTERISTICS (SC)			
Student absentee rate	12.89	18.79	11.26
	(23.34)	(23.76)	(16.17)
Age	11.39	11.01	10.94
	(1.43)	(1.32)	(1.30)
Gender	0.69	0.60	0.58
TEACHER CHARACTERISTICS (TC)			
Teacher math scores	5.91	6.45	5.95
	(2.89)	(2.88)	(2.79)
Teacher comp. scores	24.19	23.74	24.62
	(4.59)	(4.61)	(3.00)
Matric degree	0.17	0.20	0.21
Intermediate degree	0.56	0.53	0.32
Bachelors' degree	0.16	0.21	0.38
Masters' degree	0.12	0.06	0.09
Primary teacher certificate, junior vernacular, or none	0.52	0.82	0.67
Certificate of teaching (CT)	0.29	0.11	0.25
Higher certificate of teaching (HTT)	0.19	0.07	0.08
In-service training	0.48	0.05	0.45
Teacher experience	10.35	5.80	5.01
	(6.31)	(9.80)	(5.1)
Being teacher first preference	0.57	0.68	0.59
Teacher absentee rate	9.20	7.37	6.82
	(7.18)	(7.84)	(6.25)
Teacher provide private tuition	0.16	0.30	0.26
SCHOOL CHARACTERISTICS – POLICY (SP)			
Student-teacher ratio	20.02	19.63	19.87
	(12.63)	(11.45)	(8.45)
All-boys' school	0.52	-	-
All-girls' school	0.26	0.01	0.10
Student repeating class	0.05	0.02	0.04
Regular school inspection	0.88	0.69	0.64
Homework assigned regularly	0.84	0.84	0.83
Medium of instruction in mother tongue	0.53	0.19	0.23

Single-shift school	0.91	0.97	0.93
Single-grade school	0.86	0.77	0.81
Fines imposed for being absent	0.17	0.18	0.19
Report card shown to parents	0.42	0.64	0.64
Parents sign report card	0.26	0.86	0.84
Using own curriculum	-	0.13	0.13
Weekly tests	0.23	0.35	0.33
Monthly tests	0.09	0.20	0.24
Term tests	0.47	0.37	0.37
Annual tests	0.20	0.06	0.06
Primary school	0.69	0.25	0.24
Primary unit part of middle school	0.22	0.37	0.51
Primary unit part of high school	0.09	0.38	0.25
Students beaten	0.51	0.48	0.37
Extra help after school	0.69	0.68	0.62
SCHOOL CHARACTERISTICS-FACILITIES (SF)			
Desks available in classrooms	0.30	0.65	0.86
Chairs available in classrooms	0.33	0.79	0.95
Class held outside	0.32	0.04	0.01
No electricity	0.23	0.00	0.02
Good lighting	0.13	0.13	0.53
Medium lighting	0.38	0.40	0.30
Poor lighting	0.41	0.47	0.17
Washroom	0.38	0.96	1.00
Water available	0.79	1.00	0.93
Desks available for teachers	0.66	0.90	0.92
Charts	0.09	0.42	0.59
Models	0.02	0.13	0.24
Library	0.05	0.31	0.52
Chalk available	0.77	0.94	0.99
SCHOOL EVALUATION BY FIELD TEAM (SE)			
Evaluated as good	0.17	0.58	0.80
Evaluated as mixed	0.11	0.05	0.01
Evaluated as bad	0.72	0.37	0.19
Other variables			
School fee	2.73	107.25	115.40
	(4.86)	(67.89)	(55.16)
N	630	476	587

Source: SDPI survey
Note: Parentheses contain standard deviations

Table 2a: Demand for school type as selection control (binary probit with government, private, NGO = 1, else = 0)

	Government	Private	NGO
Constant	1.874	0.040	-0.128
	(1.49)	(0.12)	(0.40)
Extremely poor	13.361	-1.095*	-0.360***
	(0.48)	(4.28)	(1.64)
Poor	2.018*	-0.814*	-0.327**
	(2.86)	(-5.30)	(2.08)
Middle class	0.823**	-0.171	0.043
	(2.01)	(1.54)	(0.38)
Gender	0.751***	-0.088	-0.250*
	(1.76)	(1.25)	(3.56)
Number of school-going-age siblings	0.048	-0.043**	0.002
	(0.52)	(2.04)	(0.09)
Age	0.053	-0.029	-0.063**
	(0.52)	(1.12)	(2.37)
Fee	-0.085*	0.004*	0.006*
	(8.73)	(6.16)	(9.26)
Fee*extremely poor	-0.245	0.010*	0.003
	(0.04)	(3.62)	(1.52)
Fee*poor	-0.042***	0.006*	0.004*
	(1.78)	(5.11)	(3.88)
Fee*middle class	-0.019	-0.001**	0.003*
	(1.57)	(2.26)	(4.63)
Log-likelihood	-39.52	-889.54	-881.28
Chi-squared	2155.97*	232.36*	422.74*
N	1693	1693	1693

Source: SDPI survey.

Notes: Parentheses contain t-values

    *   Significant at least at the 1 per cent level.

    **   Significant at least at the 5 per cent level

    ***   Significant at least at the 10 per cent level.

    Rich and female are the base categories for the dummy variables.

Table 2b: Educational production function for government, private and NGO schools with sample selection (Dependent variable: Comprehension scores)

	Government	Private	NGO
FAMILY CHARACTERISTICS (FC)			
Father's education	0.041	0.039	0.074***
	(0.84)	(0.76)	(1.72)
Mother's education	0.134***	0.180*	-0.027
	(1.89)	(2.92)	(0.51)
Number of educated siblings	0.650	2.210**	0.652
	(0.77)	(2.15)	(0.74)
Parents check homework	0.226	-	0.234
	(0.51)		(0.56)
STUDENT CHARACTERISTICS (SC)			
Student absentee rate •	-0.010	-0.016	-0.013
	(1.04)	(1.47)	(1.03)
Age	0.129	0.051	-0.001
	(0.95)	(0.27)	(0.02)
Gender	0.665	-1.308*	-0.630
	(0.64)	(2.60)	-(1.19)
TEACHER CHARACTERISTICS (TC)			
Teacher marks in comprehension scores	-0.215	0.100	0.308**
	(1.58)	(0.74)	(2.31)
Intermediate degree	-8.365*	5.107**	0.088
	(4.24)	(2.74)	(0.07)
Bachelors' degree	-1.232	-2.209	1.435
	(0.58)	(0.67)	(1.16)
Masters' degree	-5.663*	6.405***	-2.177
	(2.27)	(1.65)	(1.38)
Certificate of teaching (CT)	0.135	12.031*	-0.917
	(0.07)	(4.81)	(0.77)
Higher certificate of teaching (HTT)	2.042	5.174	0.935
	(1.16)	(1.34)	(0.76)
In-service training	-1.480	-4.012**	2.422**
	(1.16)	(2.00)	(2.26)
Teacher experience	0.195*	0.250*	-0.046
	(2.99)	(4.87)	(0.37)
Being teacher first preference	1.772**	-1.899***	-0.743
	(1.94)	(1.78)	(0.75)
Teacher absentee rate	0.148	0.102	0.329*
	(1.54)	(1.39)	(3.95)
Teacher provide private tuition	2.292	-	1.139
	(1.48)		(1.44)

SCHOOL CHARACTERISTICS –
POLICY (SP)

Student-teacher ratio	-0.120**	0.073	0.038
	(2.27)	(1.15)	(0.58)
All-boys' school	0.838	-	-
	(0.59)		
All-girls' school	3.748*	-2.639	0.427
	(2.48)	(1.15)	(0.31)
Student repeating class	-0.149	1.128	-0.124
	(0.16)	(0.75)	(0.13)
Regular school inspection	-4.611**	-6.533*	-0.014
	(2.12)	(4.07)	(0.02)
Regular homework assigned	1.167**	0.463	0.345
	(1.99)	(0.71)	(0.60)
Teaching in mother tongue	-1.007	5.749*	-4.472*
	(0.60)	(2.77)	(3.44)
Single-shift school	6.285*	7.051**	-0.571
	(2.93)	(2.10)	(0.32)
Single-grade school	-1.690	0.823	0.263
	(1.29)	(0.77)	(0.28)
Fines imposed for being absent	-8.010*	-1.135	1.474***
	(4.47)	(1.04)	(1.68)
Report card shown to parents	0.738	4.724*	0.450
	(0.68)	(3.81)	(0.40)
Parents sign report card	-1.455	-	-0.632
	(1.27)		(0.63)
Using own curriculum	-	1.214	2.651***
		(0.66)	(1.89)
Weekly tests	2.141*	-0.911	-2.662*
	(2.95)	(0.84)	(2.54)
Monthly tests	0.293	-1.057	0.541
	(0.315)	(0.90)	(0.48)
Term tests	0.996	0.565	-1.136
	(1.35)	(0.57)	(1.13)
Primary school	5.260*	-5.720**	1.049
	(2.29)	(2.20)	(0.77)
Primary unit part of middle school	4.372**	-0.182	2.058
	(2.05)	(0.09)	(1.46)
Students beaten	0.038	0.707	-0.644
	(0.08)	(1.38)	(1.39)
Extra help after school	4.222*	7.237*	1.361
	(2.36)	(4.74)	(1.12)

SCHOOL CHARACTERISTICS-FACILITIES (SF)

Desks available in classrooms	1.073	0.539	-0.749
	(0.77)	(0.22)	(1.33)
Chairs available in classrooms	-2.802***	0.548	1.731
	(1.89)	(0.41)	(0.93)
Class held outside	-3.262**	-0.641	-
	(2.21)	(0.20)	-
No electricity	-4.530*	-	-
	(2.26)		
Washroom	--5.955*	-	-
	(5.55)		
Water available	-	-	-
Desks available for teachers	5.018*	-0.629	-2.652
	(3.69)	(0.25)	(1.39)
Charts	-5.298*	-2.100	-2.837
	(2.79)	(0.92)	(2.56)
Models	-	˙-0.046	0.663
		(0.03)	(0.57)
Library	0.712	-9.083*	-3.003*
	(0.29)	(5.25)	(2.65)
Chalk available	-1.715	-4.664***	-1.214
	(0.56)	(1.64)	(0.58)

SCHOOL EVALUATION BY FIELD TEAM (SE)

Evaluated as good	6.228*	6.438*	-2.305*
	(4.60)	(3.56)	(2.62)
Evaluated as mixed	7.563*	2.013**	-
	(3.30)	(0.77)	

PROVINCES

Punjab	6.016*	-8.458*	6.183*
	(3.31)	(3.11)	(3.24)
Sindh	1.279	-5.706*	10.420*
	(0.42)	(2.23)	(4.54)
NWFP	3.044	2.380	10.297
	(1.44)	(0.97)	(6.53)

STATISTICS

Lambda	-3.832*	2.833***	3.155*
	(3.23)	(1.68)	(1.97)
R bar square@	.3969	.3813	.2676
F-statistic	9.12*	7.36*	5.76*
N	630	476	587

Notes: As in Table 2a

R bar squared is only suggestive since OLS is not being used and it is therefore not bounded between 0 and 1.

Table 3: **OLS educational production function for government, private and NGO schools (Dependent variable: math scores)**

	Government	Private	NGO
Constant	4.526*	-0.674	-0.794
	(3.24)	(0.35)	(0.59)
FAMILY CHARACTERISTICS (FC)			
Father's education	0.029***	0.002	0.028**
	(1.72)	(0.1)	(1.98)
Mother's education	0.012	0.052*	-0.034***
	(0.53)	(2.75)	(1.81)
Number of educated siblings	0.230	0.503***	0.181
	(0.87)	(1.76)	(0.69)
Parents check homework	0.044	-0.147	0.055
	(0.31)	(0.97)	(0.42)
STUDENT CHARACTERISTICS (SC)			
Student absentee rate	-0.004	0.003	-0.0006
	(1.17)	(0.68)	(0.17)
Age	0.113**	0.034	-0.026
	(2.16)	(0.57)	(0.50)
Gender	0.523	0.089	0.102
	(1.27)	(0.64)	(0.67)
TEACHER CHARACTERISTICS (TC)			
Teacher math scores	-0.083	0.034	0.223*
	(1.01)	(0.57)	(2.55)
Intermediate degree	0.163	2.173*	-0.076
	(0.32)	(4.41)	(0.20)
Bachelors' degree	-1.195***	2.520*	0.524
	(1.89)	(3.10)	(1.11)
Masters' degree	-1.16**	3.308*	0.209
	(2.14)	(3.80)	(0.32)
Certificate of teaching (CT)	0.546	2.828*	0.872*
	(1.37)	(3.74)	(2.52)
Higher certificate of teaching (HTT)	2.817*	-0.137	0.384
	(5.55)	(0.88)	(0.96)
In-service training	0.366	0.634	0.416
	(1.04)	(0.15)	(0.86)
Teacher experience	-0.016	0.133*	-0.012
	(0.54)	(7.43)	(0.31)
Being teacher first preference	-0.010	0.932*	-0.447
	(0.04)	(2.76)	(1.25)
Teacher absentee rate	-0.023	-0.011	0.009
	(1.12)	(0.52)	(0.25)

Teacher provide private tuition	0.382	0.714*	0.324
	(0.87)	(2.47)	(1.24)

SCHOOL CHARACTERISTICS – POLICY (SP)

Student-teacher ratio	-0.030**	0.035**	0.081*
	(1.87)	(2.01)	(3.75)
All-boys' school	0.810	-	-
	(1.43)		
All-girls' school	-1.471*	0.471	-0.391
	(2.85)	(0.59)	(0.83)
Student repeating class	0.072	-	-
	(0.25)		
Regular school inspection	-0.753	-1.610*	0.899*
	(1.35)	(4.62)	(3.51)
Homework assigned regularly	0.283	-0.051	-0.210
	(1.42)	(0.30)	(1.17)
Medium of instruction in mother tongue	0.084	1.452**	-2.020*
	(0.19)	(2.33)	(4.43)
Single-shift school	-	-	1.675*
			(2.96)
Single-grade school	-0.780**	0.500	-0.862*
	(2.23)	(1.60)	(2.97)
Fines imposed for being absent	-0.966	-0.895*	-0.501
	(1.61)	(3.41)	(0.98)
Report card shown to parents	-0.417	0.581	-0.070
	(1.27)	(1.02)	(0.22)
Parents sign report card	-0.135	-0.312	-0.232
	(0.39)	(0.86)	(0.82)
Using own curriculum	-	-0.386	-0.039
		(0.77)	(0.08)
Weekly tests	1.03*	-0.403	-0.302
	(4.66)	(1.07)	(0.83)
Monthly tests	-0.191	-0.830**	-0.131
	(0.62)	(1.95)	(0.37)
Term tests	-0.212	-0.545	-0.486
	(0.81)	(1.60)	(1.50)
Primary school	0.461	1.975*	0.992**
	(1.15)	(3.17)	(1.99)
Primary unit part of middle school	0.211	0.813***	1.856*
	(0.38)	(1.65)	(5.44)
Students beaten	-0.056	0.303***	0.026
	(0.38)	(1.92)	(0.17)
Extra help after school	-1.569*	0.134	0.135
	(2.75)	(0.39)	(0.36)

SCHOOL CHARACTERISTICS-FACILITIES (SF)

Desks available in classrooms	-0.198	0.117	-0.255
	(0.17)	(0.15)	(0.41)
Chairs available in classrooms	0.436	1.013*	2.842*
	(1.50)	(2.50)	(4.27)
Class held outside	-0.276	0.410	-2.999***
	(0.93)	(0.51)	(1.71)
No electricity	0.134	-	-
	(0.09)		
Good lighting	-1.555***	-	-0.372
	(1.78)		(0.99)
Washroom	-0.721	-	-
	(0.87)		
Water available	2.103	-	-
	(1.56)		
Desks available for teachers	-0.544***	-1.295**	-
	(1.66)	(2.20)	
Charts	-0.826	-1.801**	-
	(1.50)	(4.12)	
Models	-0.572	4.00*	0.271
	(0.85)	(7.85)	(0.62)
Library	0.881	0.565	0.829***
	(1.45)	(1.26)	(1.64)
Chalk available	-0.538	-0.350	-
	(0.72)	(0.43)	

SCHOOL EVALUATION BY FIELD TEAM (SE)

Evaluated as good	1.977*	2.959*	-1.149**
	(4.79)	(6.72)	(3.59)
Evaluated as moderate	0.179	3.624*	-
	(0.32)	(3.19)	

PROVINCES

Punjab	2.195*	-2.475*	-2.186**
	(4.38)	(2.80)	(2.27)
Sindh	-0.271	-2.388*	0.148
	(0.42)	(2.48)	(0.17)
NWFP	2.042*	-0.459	0.513
	(3.58)	(0.52)	(0.79)
R bar square	.4653	.5305	.3096
F-statistic	12.90*	12.42*	6.97*
N	630	476	587

Source: SDPI survey.
Note: Parentheses contain t-values
  *   Significant at least at the 1 per cent level.
  **   Significant at least at the 5 per cent level
  *** Significant at least at the 10 per cent level.
  The base dummy variables are as follows: Rich for socio-economic background of families, for teacher education, the base is matric (class 10), for teacher certification, the base is PTC (primary teacher certification), for tests, the base is annual tests, for the kind of school the base is a co-educational school and for all other dummy variables 0 is the base category.

NOTES

1. Thanks are due to Haris Gazdar for comments on an earlier version of this chapter. This chapter draws on a paper using an alternative estimation technique currently under review by *Economics of Education Review*.

2. Knight and Sabot (1990) and Alderman et al. (1996) have used the raven test scores as a measure of innate ability; this test was criticized on various counts by Khan (1993).

3. He questions the implicit assumptions of additivity and homotheticity and uses instead a translog production function.

4. Prominent among these studies are Goldhaber and Brewer (1997) and Krueger (1999). Other studies are cited and reviewed by Vignoles et al. (2000) who presented an extensive discussion of methodological issues and reviewed the findings of the 'high quality' studies from the USA and UK. Other studies include Levin (2001) and Wilson (2001), and Todd and Wolpin (2003) for a methodological discussion.

5. Carnoy (1995) is a useful source on these hypotheses.

6. The sample of students is a non-random and endogenously selected sample. Using OLS is premised on the fundamental assumption that the error term is random and uncorrelated with the right hand side variables. If these right hand side variables also determine who opts to be a student in a particular type of schools, i.e. government, private, or NGO, the error term will be systematically correlated with the included right hand side variables in the model. To deal with this potential 'sample selection bias', the two-step Heckman (1976) procedure is used. The first step was to estimate a demand for school type equation by using a probit (i.e. estimating the probability of attending a particular type of school), which is reported as Annex 5.1, Table 2a. This step is used to estimate the Inverse Mill's Ratio (lambda), which removes the bias in the second step by ensuring a normal distribution of residuals for the students' cognitive skills production functions. Parental income was used as an identifying exclusion restriction. While income of parents can affect performance, Coates (2003, p. 274) indicate that parental income is now viewed as '... a poor proxy for the quality and quantity of parental input into the education process.' Such effects are more likely to be mediated by parental education. Most of the variables in the second stage regression should be included in the first stage. To avoid the multicollinearity problem, we have allowed school fees to capture these effects as a summary variable. Finally, while we run three choice models, given the similarity between private and NGO schools and our focus on government schools, the model of interest is government vs. 'non-government' schools. More important, based on our fieldwork, we found that if the parents decide not to seek admission to a government school or to take their children out of the government schools, they opted for the 'non-government' school most convenient for them. However, given that the choice models differ, the interpretation of the estimated selectivity-correction term also differs. An alternative approach, if each choice were as relevant, would be to use multinomial logit estimation [refer to Folio and Stone (1999)].

7. Parental income and school fees are included in the demand for school type equations used for the first stage selection control.

8. We have not included measures of innate ability, such as the Raven's test or other IQ tests. These tests are controversial, as earlier indicated, and so we did not administer them. In this regard, this study, like many others, suffers from a missing variable bias.

9. In most cases, significant coefficients are interpreted, unless non-significant findings are important.

10. We estimated a log-linear specification to test the robustness of the coefficients. The coefficients under the two specifications were virtually identical. Since several of the students scored a zero on one or both tests, using the log version resulted in a loss of observations and hence we opted not to use the log-linear specification even though this provided the advantage of interpreting the coefficients in terms of their percentage impact on test performance.

11. The magnitudes are mentioned in the text when notable, but only when the coefficient is statistically significant. Given the very large number of variables, many of them binary, multicollinearity was inevitable and variables had to be dropped using a time consuming sequential method to avoid singularity. A less time consuming option would have been to use a technique like the Lagrange multiplier test to omit variables. However, this was avoided both because the lack of significance is often instructive when repeated across specifications and because the omissions are rule-based (arbitrary) rather than theory-based. Another related difficult decision confronted was the loss of observations in deciding to include key variables like the education of parents. In all, 354 observations were lost across the three specifications by school type. We excluded the key variables, and re-estimated the equations with all observations and found that the main results reported in this paper did not change, although the size of the coefficients naturally varied somewhat. In this regard, we once again view the findings as stable.

12. As reported in Annex 5.1, Table 1, the monthly fee in government schools was Rs 2.73 compared to Rs 107.25 and Rs 115.40 in private and NGO schools respectively. The high monthly fee in the NGO schools was a surprise for us, although the communities regarded them as private schools. However, they had much more active policies in place for subsidizing poor students than private schools (also refer to chapter 2 on this issue).

13. Comprehension and math test scores for teachers were used as explanatory variables. The comprehension test for teachers was taken from an IFPRI project on education in rural Pakistan [Alderman et al., (1995)], whereas a math test from the same project was adapted based on pre-tests.

14. The coefficient for NGO schools is negative and multicollinearity is a likely explanation for this and some other implausible results we report.

15. Pakistan has currently a national language and four main provincial languages, but linguists have identified fifty-two languages spoken in this geographical entity.

16. As reported in Annex 5.1, Table 1, beatings were prevalent in 51 per cent government schools, 48 per cent private schools, and 37 per cent NGO schools respectively.

17. One way around the multicollinearity problem is using indices. However, the problem is that assigned weights are often arbitrary and it is difficult to identify the policy significance of the various components of the index.

18. However, one needs to bear in mind that 80 per cent NGO schools were ranked as successful.

6

Rationality in public sector salary scales[1]

6.1. Introduction

Public sector salary scales in Pakistan are explicitly based on fixed rules such as linking salaries to educational qualifications and experience.[2] This applies also to the remuneration of rural school teachers. Efficiency would require that salaries be tied to productivity. Of course, there may be a hidden or overt rationality in fixed rules, i.e. such fixed rules may actually reward productivity and hence be efficient and hence 'rational'. The purpose of this chapter is to empirically identify the presence or absence of rationality in the public sector salary scales of rural teachers.

The fixed salary rule for teachers' salaries is implicitly justified by the human capital theory.[3] The fixed salary rule views educational qualifications and experience, the two central human capital variables, as enhancing productivity which in turn is expected to be rewarded by a higher salary.[4] The relevant questions are therefore the following: What represents teacher productivity or effectiveness? Does the teacher incentive structure reward teacher effectiveness?[5]

We define teacher effectiveness in terms of the impact of teacher's skills on student cognitive skills.[6] The advantage of this definition is that it is specific and quantifiable. Our data sets are rich enough to allow us to investigate these issues. An earlier data set was used by Behrman et al. (1997) to establish that teacher cognitive skills are significantly and positively associated with student cognitive skills.[7] In chapter 5, the comparative data set used throughout the book is utilized to show that higher teacher scores in math and comprehension enhance student math and comprehension scores for NGO schools. In this chapter, we therefore concentrate on the second issue of exploring if there is a link between teacher effectiveness and teacher incentives. We also use the comparative data set to investigate if rural teacher salaries in the private and NGO sectors follow similar practice to the government sector to get another perspective on this 'rationality hypothesis'.

Ballou and Podgursky (1992) looked at the structure of pay in private schools and the lessons these provided for public schools in the USA. However, they estimated wage functions but did not have access to data that would enable them to estimate the impact of different variables, including educational qualifications and experience, on cognitive skills. Goldhaber and Brewer (1998) empirically demonstrated that only subject-specific higher educational qualifications for teachers contribute significantly to enhancing student scores in the same subject, although modestly so. Based on this finding, they conclude that there is a justification for salary jumps based on higher educational qualifications only for those teaching that subject and not for an across the board increase.

We have taken this investigation further by first identifying more broadly the variables that impact teacher cognitive skills, given the positive association of teacher cognitive skills and student cognitive skills. Following that, we investigate what impact these variables have on salaries. The conceptual framework is spelled out in section 6.2, the data described in section 6.3, findings are reported in section 6.4, and we end with a summary.

6.2. Conceptual framework

Our conceptual framework is premised on the existence of a set of associations as identified by the teacher cognitive skills production function and teacher wage functions. Equation 1 below is a cognitive skills production function and the purpose of estimating it is to see if teacher education and experience enhance teacher cognitive skills. Equation 2 represents a teacher wage equation and the purpose of estimating it is to see how closely tied the salary structure is to education and experience. If education and experience enhance teacher cognitive skills and they are also positively associated with wages, we can infer that there is some rationality in the salary structure.[8]

(1) CS = CS(G,R,PSA,ED,EX,P,TT),
(2) W = E(G,R,PSA,CS,ED,EX,P,TT, HT),
where,

> CS is cognitive skills;
> W is wages;
> G is gender;
> R is region (district as described below);
> PSA is pre-school ability;
> ED is educational qualifications;
> EX is experience;
> P is grade or performance at the highest level of schooling attained;
> TT includes pre-service and in-service teacher training;
> HT is whether or not the teacher interviewed was the head teacher

Equation 1 represents a cognitive skills production function.[9] The production of base cognitive skills is embedded on the right hand side and proxied by educational attainment (ED) and performance in the highest level of schooling attained (P). Other inputs such as teacher training and experience can be viewed to add to the base teacher cognitive skills.

6.3. Data and variables

Starting in 1986, the International Food Policy Research Institute (IFPRI), under the auspices of the Pakistan Ministry of Food and Agriculture, administered a multi-purpose survey to a panel of 800 plus rural households containing over 7000 individuals drawn from three poor districts and one relatively prosperous one (one from each of Pakistan's four provinces). The districts of Attock, Badin and Dir were selected on the basis of production and infrastructure indices.[10] Faisalabad as the relatively prosperous district was selected for contrast. Human capital modules were administered in the spring of 1989, the tenth round of the survey. Within districts, village clusters and households were chosen using a stratified random sample. There were 102 rural government schools in the sample of schools, and the school data set was based on linking household members to proximate schools. Once schools were identified, a separate data set was generated for 579 primary and middle school teachers. Our total sample of teachers was 611 because we also had teachers in the household sub-sample of 2800. The teacher data set is the focus of attention for this study.

The variables that are unique to this data set merit some elaboration. The measure of cognitive skills (CS) was generated by administering (in the regional language) to every person in our sample more than 10 years old (including teachers), and with at least four years of schooling, tests of literacy and numeracy specially designed by the Educational Testing Service, Princeton.[11]

To obtain a measure of pre-school ability (PSA), we administered Raven's (1956) Colored Progressive Matrices (CPM), a test of reasoning ability that involves matching patterns, to everybody in the sample 10 years of age or older.[12] The test is designed so that formal schooling does not influence performance, though performance may reflect early childhood environment as well as innate capacity. The disaggregate distributions for Dir, Attock, Faisalabad and Badin are very similar. Since educational attainment differs substantially across regions, this similarity is consistent with the presumption that educational attainment does not influence performance on the Raven's CPM test. The comparative data sets this book is primarily based on and which are also used for this chapter are described in Appendix 1.

6.4. Estimation and analysis

There are two components to the estimation and analysis of rationality in rural teacher salary structure. First, we analyze whether rural public sector teacher salaries are consistent with teacher effectiveness. Second, we see if similar practices prevail in the private and NGO sectors.

6.4.1. Rationality in rural teacher salary structure

Teacher cognitive skills production function

The question to be explored in this sub-section is whether education and experience, among other variables, enhance teachers' productivity? We found significant selectivity in the production of cognitive skills, and so the math and comprehension production functions reported are corrected for sample selection.[13] We accepted the null of equality of variances by gender (which ruled out a Chow test) and started with a full set of interaction terms. A high goodness of fit in the first step probit estimation is important for the second step. The likelihood ratio test statistic for the null, that the slope coefficients are zero, is 219.8 and is rejected at an extremely low level of significance. The supply equation correctly predicts the probability of becoming a teacher 92 per cent of the time as shown in Annex 6, Table 1. The cognitive skills production functions are reported as Annex 6, Table 2.

As might be expected, pre-school ability is positively and significantly associated with the production of both math and comprehension cognitive skills. All reported levels of education contribute significantly to math skills and comprehension skills. This provides some support for basing the salary structure on educational qualifications. Experience does not appear to matter in either case. We do not reject the hypotheses that certification as a teacher contributes to math skills while in-service training contributes to comprehension skills. Thus while there is likely to be much scope for improvement, the pre-service teacher training programs in Pakistan do not appear to be completely ineffective as is often believed to be the case.[14]

Individuals selected by the boards externally grade the national board exams, which come under the jurisdiction of various universities. Candidates can generally earn a first, second, or third division or a pass if they are successful. The division achieved is widely used in public and private sector hiring decisions both as a formal screening criteria in job advertisements and as a selection criteria for otherwise equally qualified candidates. We find that a second division, but not a first division, is a significant predictor of teacher math and comprehension scores relative to a third division or pass for both genders. Thus the cautious use of performance as relevant hiring information is justified.

The teacher wage functions

We did not find lambda to be statistically significant in either the male or female wage function, estimated as a bi-variate probit with sample selection, which suggests that selection bias was not important. As in the case of the educational production functions, gender dummies are used with interaction terms to identify significant differences. While rural public sector school education in Pakistan comes under provincial jurisdiction, the service provided varies little across provinces.

However, regional dummies are used to control for fixed effects in the wage equations reported in Annex 6, Table 3.

A high proportion of the total wage variance is explained by the earnings functions [R2 (.67)]. Despite rigidities in the salary structure, there are important insights that emerge from estimating the wage equations. Central to this chapter is exploring the direct and indirect reward for teacher productivity. The direct reward would be higher earnings based on higher cognitive skills. The indirect reward would be higher earnings associated with teacher characteristics that produce higher cognitive skills. We established in Annex 6, Table 2 that teacher education and teacher certification were positively associated with teacher cognitive skills. Thus, rationality in the incentive structure would require that higher earnings be associated with these characteristics.

The earning function estimated in Annex 6, Table 3 allows us to explore these direct and indirect associations of teacher productivity and earnings. Math, but not comprehension, skills are positively associated with earnings, but the size of the coefficient is very small. Therefore exploring the indirect reward to teacher productivity assumes greater importance. The 'pure' human capital variables, i.e. education and experience do in a broad sense have a positive impact on earnings. However, some qualifications are in order.

First, those with an intermediate, bachelors' and masters' degree earn more than those who possessed only a matric degree. Since these higher degrees contribute to higher cognitive skills, there is justification for the higher wages. However, we did not find a progressively higher contribution to cognitive skills with educational qualification and so inferring higher teacher productivity with a higher degree is not possible. Second, while we did not find that experience contributed to cognitive skills, experience is rewarded in the form of a higher salary. Third, we found that performance on the last degree had an impact on cognitive skills but has no association with teacher salary.

The other important human capital variable is teacher training. After each of the three initial education levels, there are options to move to vocational tracks. The primary teacher certificate (PTC) is a nine-month vocational option after matriculation. After the intermediate level, students can opt either for the professional or technical streams, which once again include pre-service teacher training. Those wanting to teach middle school are required to earn a teachers' certificate (CT), which again entails nine months of training.

Most descriptive accounts suggest that teacher training in Pakistan is not cost-effective. The quality of pre-service teacher instruction is described as poor by both government [*Seventh Five Year Plan*, (pp. 359-60), National Education Policy, 1998–2000 (1998, pp. 47-8] and non-government sources [Warick et al. (1991) and The World Bank, (1988, p. 26)]. In-service training appears to be taken lightly and government sources describe these courses as being attended 'in a holiday mood' and of poor quality.[15]

Even so, attaining teachers' certification is positively and significantly associated with wages while the reverse is the case for in-service training. Annex 6, Table 2 showed that teacher certification significantly contributed to producing higher math skills while in-service training contributed to producing higher comprehension skills. The negative association of in-service training with earnings is because individuals needing in-service training are probably on a slower track or holding *ad hoc* positions. Our analysis provides support for this conjecture. When in-service training is substituted by temporary teachers (temp) and the interaction of temp and in-service training, the coefficient of the latter is negative and highly significant.

Thus, within the set salary structure, there is in reality a dual track. On the fast track, a teacher with the right educational and teaching qualifications starts with a regular appointment (tenured). Those who do not fully qualify can be given *ad hoc* positions if there is a shortage of teachers, which has been the case in rural areas. *Ad hoc* positions can be regularized on the recommendation of the head teacher and the district educational officer (DEO) in the annual review of teachers. One condition for a positive recommendation for regularization is having successfully met the required qualifications while in service. Since teachers can stay *ad hoc* for a long time, significant salary differences could in principle emerge, particularly when a teacher reaches the upper end of a salary scale.[16]

One last point relates to the higher salary of the head-teacher.[17] We used a probit model (not reported) to investigate the determinants of promotion. The most striking finding is that math skills are inversely associated with promotion while the reverse was true for comprehension skills. Other rural wage-workers' wage functions are also reported, since these occupations could be representing the opportunity cost for the teachers.[18]

The descriptive statistics for the second data sets are reported in Annex 6, Table 4. This reports data by gender disaggregation, and also by institutional disaggregation (i.e. for government, private and NGO schools). Some striking findings are that the public sector teachers on average earn much more than private sector (twice as much) and NGO sector (35 per cent more) teachers. They have higher experience and qualifications and have received more training, but the performance on the math and comprehensive tests is very similar to the private and NGO sector teachers. Interestingly, the percentage of female teachers (60 per cent) is much higher in the public sector than the private (37 per cent) and NGO (14 per cent) sectors. This is a result of deliberate public sector education policy to encourage teaching by females at the primary level because they are perceived to be less harsh than male teachers.

Annex 6, Table 5 reports wage functions for government, NGO, and private schools for the more recent comparative data sets.[19] The most significant finding in Annex 6, Table 5 is that the F-statistic was completely insignificant in the government wage equation compared to the private and NGO sector equations. Beyond that, not surprisingly, experience was the only significant variable in the public sector wage equation. Thus most of the variation in the pooled regression in column 5 comes from across pooled types and not from within the government school sector. The positive and significant coefficient for experience indicate, as one would expect, that public sector teacher salaries are not responsive to teachers' productive characteristics but set on the basis of mandated rules. By comparison, NGO and private sector teacher salaries are responsive to qualifications. However, even here, math and comprehension test scores do not play a role.[20]

Teacher's qualifications and experience are the main significant predictors accounting for higher earnings. The private sector wage function has better explanatory power and it shows average expected earnings of teachers with an intermediate, bachelors' and masters' degree of 79 per cent, 123 per cent and 121 per cent more respectively than matriculate teachers. Experience counts, and one year additional experience adds about 3 and 5 per cent to the mean expected salary in private and NGO schools respectively.

Summary and recommendations

The object of this chapter was to explore the existence of some 'rationality' in the public sector salary structure for rural teachers. The salary structure is stated to be tied to teacher educational qualifications and experience, and this was empirically confirmed. Such a salary structure could be justified on efficiency grounds if indeed it could be demonstrated that educational qualifications and experience are positively associated with teacher effectiveness. Teacher effectiveness is defined as teacher cognitive skills in math and comprehension. The justification of viewing these skills as a measure of teacher effectiveness is the positive and significant association of teacher cognitive skills and student cognitive skills on the same tests.

For the public sector, the IFPRI (International Food Policy Research Institute) data sets indicate that higher educational qualifications are positively associated with teacher effectiveness. Thus, there appears to be an overall rationality in the rural teacher incentive structure. However, the rigidity of the system becomes evident at closer examination. First, while experience is rewarded with higher wages and promotion, there is no association of experience with teacher cognitive skills. Second, wages progressively increase with higher degrees while there is no linear association of the level of the degree and teacher cognitive skills. Third, performance in the last degree is associated with higher teacher cognitive skills but not with higher earnings.

These findings suggest that rigid public sector salary rules have severe limitations and are unable to adequately reward those that produce the best results. This becomes more evident from the findings evident from the comparative data sets used throughout this book that contrast rural public schools with private and NGO sector schools. While private and NGO sector teacher salaries are responsive to qualifications, this is not at all the case in the rural public sector.

There are no simple solutions. However, interestingly, the military in Pakistan routinely tests officers for promotion and the less able are passed over or weeded out. Moving to a test-based system for confirming teachers from temporary to permanent and for promoting them from junior to senior teachers would be a step towards ensuring good teaching, although currently the capacity to do this does not exist.

Various sound proposals to reform teacher training in Pakistan have been made.[21] Apart from these, building in a positive incentive in the salary structure to encourage teachers to enhance their skills may work by inducing greater effort and productivity among existing teachers.

Personal experience and observation indicates that teaching is a gift and not necessarily found among those with higher qualifications. This gift could be honed and polished with good training. However, to encourage those who have such a gift to become and stay on as teachers, the government would need to experiment with a much more decentralized reward system rather than rely on rigid rules. In this regard, a better outcome may be possible by tapping in to the special knowledge of communities and parents regarding teacher performance via empowered school management committees (refer to chapter 3). In view of the current attempt at devolution of power to the grassroots level in Pakistan, this suggestion is much more practical than it would otherwise have been.

References

Alderman, H., J. R. Behrman, D. R. Ross and R. H. Sabot, 1991, 'Decomposing the Gender Gap in Cognitive Skills in a Poor Rural Economy', *Journal of Human Resources*, Volume 31, No. 4, pp. 229-54.

Ballou, D. and M. Podgurski, 1992, 'The Structure of Pay in Private Schools: Are There Lessons for Public Schools?' University of Massachusets, Amhest, mimeo.

Behrman, J., and V. Lavy, 1995, 'Production Functions, Input Allocations and Unobservables: The Case of Child Health and Schooling Success', University of Pennsylvania, Philadelphia, draft.

Behrman, J., S. R. Khan, D. Ross and D. Sabot, 1997, 'School Quality and Cognitive Achievement Production: A Case Study for Rural Pakistan', *Economics of Education Review*, Volume 16, No. 2.

Behrman, J. R., S. R. Khan, D. R. Ross, and R. H. Sabot, 1993, 'Teacher Effectiveness and Incentives in Rural Pakistan', Human Capital Accumulation in Post-Green Revolution Pakistan Project, International Food Policy Research Institute, Washington DC.

Boissiere, M., J. B. Knight, and R. H. Sabot, 1985, 'Earnings, Schooling, Ability and Cognitive Skills', *American Economic Review*, Vol. 75.

Glewwe, P., 1990, 'Schooling, Skills and the Returns to Education: An Econometric Exploration Using Data from Ghana', Washington DC: World Bank, draft.

Glewwe, P., 1994, 'Are Rates of Return to Schooling Estimated from Wage Data Relevant Guides for Government Investments in Education? Evidence from a Developing Country', LSMS Working Paper No. 76, Washington DC.: World Bank.

Goldhaber, D. D., and D. J. Brewer, 1998, 'When Should we Reward Degrees for Teachers', *Phi Delta Kappan Magazine*, October 1, 1998.

Government of Pakistan, 1987, *Seventh Five Year Plan (1988-93) and Perspective Plan (1988–2003) Report of the Sub-Working Group on Primary Education* (Islamabad: Planning Commission).

Government of Pakistan, n.d., *Ninth Five Year Plan (1998–2003): Education and Training* (Islamabad: Planning Commission, draft chapter, mimeo).

Heckman, J., 1976, 'The Common Structure of Statistical Models of Truncation, Sample Selection and Limited Dependent Variables,' *Annals of Economic and Social Measurement*, 5a.

Khan, M. A., 1993, 'Reports and Papers Prepared Under the Provisions of HRD Component of the Pakistan Project: Comments and Queries', Baltimore, The Johns Hopkins University, mimeo.

Khan, S. R., 2003, 'Rationality in Public Sector Salary Scales: The Case of Rural Teachers in Pakistan', *Education Economics*, Vol. 10, No. 3.

Knight, J. B. and R. H. Sabot, 1990, *Education, Productivity and Inequality: The East African Natural Experiment* (New York: Oxford University Press).

Lookheed, M. E. and A. M. Vesspoor et al., 1990, *Improving Primary Education in Developing Countries: A Review of Policy Options*, World Conference for Education for all, Bangkok, March 5-9, 1990, draft.

Schultz, T. P., 'Education Investments and Returns', 1988, in eds. H. Chenery and T. N. Srinivasan, *Handbook of Development Economics*, Vol. 1. (New York: Elsevier Science Publishers).

Warick, D. P., H. Nauman and F. Reimers, 1991, 'Is Teacher Training Worth the Investment?' Harvard University, BRIDGES Project, mimeo.

World Bank, 1988, *Pakistan Education Sector Strategy Review*, Washington DC., Report No. 7110-PAK.

Annex 6

Table 1: Binary probit (teacher = 1, non-teacher = 0)

Variables	Coefficient	T-Stat	Significance
Constant	-0.9030	-1.41	0.14
Attock	-0.6269	-2.25	0.02
Faisalabad	-1.3632	-4.30	0.00
Dir	0.0703	0.25	0.80
Pre-school ability	0.0661	3.69	0.00
Gender	2.3962	5.57	0.00
Household head	0.1102	0.52	0.60
Distance to work	0.0298	0.57	0.57
Born in village	-1.7334	-6.08	0.00
Math	0.0715	4.12	0.00
Comprehension	-0.0118	-0.74	0.46
Wage	0.0002	1.18	0.24
Log-liklihood	-100.95		
Chi-squared (11)		219.80	0.00
N	559		
Correct predictions	92%		

Table 2: **Teacher cognitive skills production function adjusting for sample selection.**

Variables	Math		Comprehension	
	Coefficient	T-Stat.	Coefficient	T-Stat
Constant	10.3900*	3.77	16.0430*	7.00
Attock	0.3141	0.18	0.8114	0.67
Faisalabad	1.5998	1.03	2.7174**	2.12
Dir	-3.9171*	-3.58	-5.5994*	-5.86
Pre-school ability	0.1775**	2.21	0.1117***	1.69
Gender	-7.1691*	-5.63	-10.9810*	-3.91
Intermediate	3.2729*	3.45	2.1124*	2.46
Bachelors'	2.9199*	3.04	1.7197**	1.97
Masters'	3.6637*	2.93	2.1594***	1.89
First	1.5927	1.16	0.1109	0.93
Second	2.6324*	2.71	2.4600*	2.80
Experience	0.0521	1.20	-0.0416	-1.08
Teacher cert.	6.0941*	5.32	0.3806	0.35
In-service trn.	-0.8138	-0.96	2.1051*	2.48
Gender*Attock	-5.0262**	-1.96		
Gender *cert.			9.2776*	3.08
Gender *in-service trn			-4.0960**	-2.23
Lambda	-12.259*	-4.20	-6.9430*	-3.44
R bar sq.	.40		.20	
F[14,564]/[16,562]	21.30*		8.09*	
N	457		457	
Math/comp. (mean/sd)	21.63	8.71	20.40	7.61

Notes: 1. The base categories are Badin (for region), male, matric and below for education (only 3.5% of the teachers had only a primary or middle degree), third division or pass (for performance), non-unionized, no teacher certificate and no in-service training.

2. Using the Breusch-Pagan test, we rejected the null of homoscedasticity and the coefficients reported have been corrected for heteroscedasticity.

3. *, **, *** represent significance at least at the 1 per cent, 5 per cent and 10 per cent levels respectively.

4. For variable definitions, see text.

Table 3: **Rural teacher and other rural worker wage functions (dependent variable is log of wages)**

Variable	Teachers		Wage-workers	
	Coefficient	T-Stat	Coefficient	T-Stat
Constant	6.8350*	77.54	6.3530*	70.93
Attock	0.0377	1.39	0.0539	1.45
Faisalabad	0.0063	0.17	0.0024	0.06
Dir	0.1048*	3.65	0.0698**	2.16
Pre-school ability	0.0005	0.31	0.0016	0.63
Gender	0.0526	-0.94	0.1417*	2.79
Intermediate	0.0573*	3.20	0.0985*	3.55
Bachelors'	0.1745*	5.28	0.2111*	6.29
Masters'	0.3014*	7.11	0.3082*	6.08
Math	0.0045*	2.58	0.0043***	1.88
Comprehension	-0.0018	-1.18	0.0028	1.23
First	-0.0400	-1.30		
Second	-0.0266	-1.15		
Experience	0.0350*	10.29	0.0398*	
Expsq	-0.0003*	-3.35	-0.0004*	
Head-teacher	0.1604*	3.96		
Teacher cert.	0.0915*	2.73		
In-service trn.	-0.0827*	-3.80		
Teacher union	-0.1410**	-2.40		
Gender*Bachelors'	0.1328**	2.11		
Teacher			0.2131*	3.72
R bar sq.	.67		.58	
F[19,437]/[13,579]	50.05*		48.21*	
N	457		593	
Wage (Mean/sd)	1579.2/	672.5	1530.8/	1019.9

Notes: As in Annex 6, Table 2.

Table 4: Descriptive statistics

	All	Male	Female	Govt.	Private	NGO
Gender	0.37	-	-	0.60	0.37	0.14
	(0.49)			(0.49)	(0.49)	(0.35)
Matric or Middle	0.15	0.10	0.17	0.12	0.19	0.14
	(0.36)	(0.31)	(0.38)	(0.32)	(0.39)	(0.35)
Intermediate	0.43	0.37	0.47	0.47	0.47	0.37
	(0.50)	(0.49)	(0.50)	(0.50)	(0.50)	(0.49)
Bachelors'	0.29	0.31	0.27	0.26	0.23	0.37
	(0.45)	(0.47)	(0.45)	(0.44)	(0.43)	(0.49)
Masters'	0.12	0.19	0.01	0.16	0.01	0.12
	(0.33)	(0.39)	(0.28)	(0.37)	(0.29)	(0.32)
Certificate of teaching (CT)	0.20	0.17	0.22	0.26	0.01	0.26
	(0.40)	(0.38)	(0.42)	(0.44)	(0.29)	(0.44)
Bachelors' or masters' education certificate	0.13	0.23	0.01	0.28	0.005	0.01
	(0.34)	(0.42)	(0.26)	(0.45)	(0.21)	(0.26)
Primary teachers certificate (PTC) or Junior Vernacular (JV)	0.28	0.35	0.23	0.47	0.21	0.16
	(0.45)	(0.48)	(0.43)	(0.50)	(0.41)	(0.37)
In service training (IST)	0.35	0.40	0.32	0.51	0.01	0.47
	(0.48)	(0.49)	(0.47)	(0.51)	(0.26)	(0.50)
Comprehension	23.57	23.87	23.38	23.12	23.09	24.49
	(4.52)	(4.27)	(4.69)	(4.73)	(5.30)	(3.27)
Math	5.79	6.77	5.21	5.28	6.23	5.86
	(2.92)	(2.77)	(2.86)	(3.05)	(2.95)	(2.73)
Teacher experience	6.62	8.19	5.70	9.95	5.40	4.47
	(7.35)	(7.66)	(7.05)	(5.75)	(9.72)	(4.51)
Teacher salary	2,561.40	3,114.94	2,233.37	3,567.40	1,800.00	2,316.67
	(2,232.14)	(2,353.63)	(2,103.48)	(1,537.09)	(2,378.85)	(2,339.29)

Note: Parentheses contain standard deviations.

Table 5: Total, NGO, private sector and government teacher wage functions

	NGO	Private	Government	Total
Constant	7.6593	5.632*	7.9858*	6.3370*
	(11.75)	(16.14)	(27.87)	(25.30)
Intermediate	0.0941	0.7949*	0.0749	0.3444*
	(0.28)	(5.03)	(0.73)	(2.52)
Bachelors'	0.8734*	1.2317*	0.3776	0.8447*
	(2.59)	(5.30)	(1.30)	(5.09)
Masters'	0.3697	1.2070*	0.1062	0.5883*
	(1.27)	(4.28)	(0.24)	(3.59)
Certificate of teaching (CT)	-0.1404	-0.6375*	-0.1625	-0.2619*
	(0.79)	(3.20)	(1.38)	(2.54)
Higher teaching certificates	0.3208	0.9585	-0.0762	0.0108
	(1.25)	(1.51)	(0.20)	(0.06)
In-service training	0.1132	0.1406	0.0391	0.1286
	(0.60)	(0.60)	(0.65)	(1.37)
Experience	0.0500**	0.0335*	0.0197*	0.0285*
	(2.43)	(11.14)	(2.45)	(7.68)
Math	0.0381	0.0147	0.0049	0.0392**
	(0.96)	(0.56)	(0.378)	(2.37)
Comprehesion	-0.0463***	0.0165	-0.0073	-0.0039
	(1.77)	(1.03)	(0.58)	(0.36)
Gender	0.2237	-0.1046	-0.0299	-0.06
	(0.59)			
	(0.70)			
	(0.40)			
	(0.50)			
Government	-	-	-	0.9490*
				(8.01)
NGO	-	-	-	0.3503*
				(2.39)
R bar sq	0.24	0.59	0.06	0.54
F [10, 32]	2.31**	7.10*	1.27	F[12,116] = 13.73*
N	43	43	43	129

Notes: 1. The base categories are matric (class 10) for teacher qualifications, primary teacher certificate for teacher training certification, for female teachers and private sector in school type for the aggregate equation.
2. *, **, ***, represent significance at least at the 1 per cent, 5 per cent and 10 per cent levels respectively.
3. Experience squared was insignificant in all cases.

NOTES

1. This chapter is based on Khan (2003).
2. For example, the draft chapter on education, written for the Ninth Five Year Plan (n.d., p. 22), states that 'Pay scales of teachers will be linked with their qualifications', and public sector salary scales link salary increments to experience.
3. Knight and Sabot (1990, chp. 13) model public sector wage determination. See Schultz (1988) for a comprehensive review article on human capital theory and also chapter 4 for a critique.
4. Salary scales within broad categories can be calibrated to respond to merit or distinction given reasonable monitoring and enforcement costs.
5. The draft chapter on education and training for the Ninth Five Year Plan, Government of Pakistan (n.d., p. 22) also proposes the use of moral incentives such as awards and medals.
6. Cognitive skills are defined by scores in math and comprehension tests.
7. The data sets are described in some detail in section 6.3 and Appendix 1. Here, the teacher-student association is identified. First, households were selected via stratified random sampling. The proximate schools (102) that children within those households attended and 579 teachers of these schools were then identified for data collection. At the primary and middle level, it is possible to link a teacher with a particular class and this was done, i.e. these students are taught by only one teacher. No minimum time requirement for a student to have been taught by a particular teacher was established, as should have been done, to weed out new teachers who were not likely to have much impact on the student's cognitive skills. However, since the mean teacher experience for primary and middle school for the sample was 10.21 (s.d. 4.51) and 12.33 (s.d. 2.44) respectively, the problem of new teachers is likely to have been small.
8. The reason for including a number of variables in both equations is not to model the direct and indirect effect of these variables on teacher salaries but to avoid the missing variable bias. Thus, gender is in the CS equation because there could be a systematic difference in performance by gender. It is also in the wage equation because there could be gender discrimination. The original paper that this chapter developed from explored gender wage discrimination using the IFPRI data set and did not find evidence of systematic gender discrimination in salaries against female teachers in the government sector. On the contrary, we found evidence of discrimination in favor of female teachers. We conjectured that this was consistent with the special effort being made by the Government of Pakistan at that time to attract and retain female teachers in rural areas. Refer to Behrman, Khan, Ross and Sabot (1993).
9. For a discussion of educational production functions, refer to chapter 5, section 5.2.
10. District and region is used interchangeably in this chapter.
11. Knight and Sabot (1990), who originally used these tests, discuss them extensively. Both the math and comprehension tests have been used successfully in research in schooling. For some examples refer to Boissiere, Knight and Sabot (1985), Glewwe (1990), Glewwe (1994), and Behrman and Lavy (1994). Both variables have been

shown to be positively correlated with wages and other indicators of productivity. For more details on the specific use of these tests in rural Pakistan, see Alderman, Behrman, Ross and Sabot (1991).

12. Since the tests were administered to people 10 years and older, it might be more accurate to view these tests as measuring ability that is independent of schooling. Since such phraseology is cumbersome, we continue to refer to these test results as measuring pre-school ability. See Khan (1993) for a critique of the Raven's score indicator.

13. The sample of teachers is a non-random and endogeneously selected sample. Using OLS is premised on the fundamental assumption that the error term is random and uncorrelated with the right hand side variables. If these right hand side variables also determine who opts to be a teacher, the error term will be systematically correlated with the included right hand side variables in the model. To deal with this potential 'sample selection bias', the two-step Heckman (1976) procedure is used. A data set was constructed by using gender, region, Raven pre-school ability test scores and cognitive skills test scores as controls to merge wage-workers from the household data set with the teacher data set. The first step was to estimate a teacher supply equation by using a probit (i.e estimating the probability of becoming a teacher), which is reported as Annex 6, Table 1. This step is used to estimate the Inverse Mill's Ratio (lambda), which removes the bias in the second step by ensuring a normal distribution of residuals for the teacher cognitive skills and wage functions. 'Born in village' is used as an identifying exclusion restriction since it is highly significant in the probit and there is no reason to suppose it should effect cognitive skills, conditional on being a teacher.

14. A teacher's certificate contributes 6.1 points to math skills, which is about 28 per cent of mean math scores, and in-service training contributes 2.1 points to comprehension skills, which is about 10 per cent of mean comprehension scores.

15. Government of Pakistan, (1987, p. 62) and (n.d., p. 22).

16. The federal and provincial governments approved a 'move-over' plan which allowed the continuation of annual increments beyond the ceiling for a particular grade even without a formal promotion to the next grade.

17. The variation in the teacher union variable was a surprise. All teachers are expected to be part of some association so it is a surprise that 15.5 per cent said they were not. It is possible that those with a lower salary are indicating dissatisfaction with the ineffectiveness of unions by not claiming their membership.

18. The main non-teacher rural occupations reflected in the sample include general labor, farm workers, watchmen, messengers, factory workers, artisans, cooks, drivers, domestics, brick-layers, clerical workers, and salesmen.

19. These equations are not exactly comparable with Annex 6, Table 3 since data on all the variables were not available.

20. As a purely predictive exercise, the salary impact of a one standard deviation (s.d.) increase in math and comprehension scores was computed for three school types. Thus a one s.d. increase in math scores would lead to a 1.5, 11 and 8.4 per cent increase respectively in mean salary in the public, private and NGO sectors. A one s.d. increase for comprehension scores indicate a decline of 1 and 14 per cent in government and NGO mean salary but a 4.4 per cent increase in private sector salary.

21. World Bank (1988, pp. 27-31). For a general review of teacher training, see Lockheed and Vesspoor (1990).

Conclusion

This book is mainly about a comparative assessment of government, private, and NGO schools in rural Pakistan to derive lessons for basic education. To procure first-hand information on rural government, private, and NGO schools, our research design started with a sampling frame of NGO schools and picked the closest private and government schools to minimize geographical differences. Even so, in some cases, the closest private school could only be found in a semi-urban area. Since government primary schools are formal and run five classes, we had to exclude a large number of non-formal NGO programs from our universe to ensure we were comparing like with like. We utilized three two-person teams of highly qualified (master's level) enumerators with prior field experience. On reaching a village, they simultaneously set about executing the research plan for a particular school type.

Students and teachers were tested for math and comprehension and a randomly selected number of students were followed back to the household to get detailed household information. They also filled in a school facility questionnaire and held focus group discussions with the community and with parents and teachers to determine if a school management committee (SMC) or parent-teacher association (PTA) existed. Based on these instruments that took one or two days to complete, each team wrote a field report following a prescribed format developed during the pre-tests. The field team also graded schools into successful, unsuccessful, or in-between. The criteria adopted was test results but also their observation of student discipline and confidence, teacher motivation and dedication, quality of physical facilities and supplies, nature of management and whether or not the students and teachers tried to cheat in the tests.

Overall, our findings are that government primary schools need urgent reform to deliver good schooling. This finding is not new for any educationist in Pakistan, though our careful documentation in the various chapters on various aspects of this failing should provide them with valuable information. We have summarized these findings and relevant contextual policy recommendations at the end of each chapter and therefore these are not reproduced here. Instead, we review what we believe to be the main findings and then turn to speculating on broader issues regarding the importance of education and why Pakistan has made such slow progress in this regard.

Policy makers in Pakistan were correctly persuaded that parental and community participation was a missing ingredient in making rural public schooling a success. Experience the world over showed parents and communities, rather than the rural schooling bureaucracy of school evaluators, assistant education officers and district education officers, as the real stakeholders. Thus teachers should be interacting with the real stakeholders rather than a remote educational bureaucracy whose incentives are not linked with the provision of effective schooling. However, as in the case of other well-meaning reforms, the key to success is conceptual clarity and effective implementation. The attempt to engender parental and community participation in rural schooling has been a singular failure and it is instructive to learn why.

Our research shows that successful schooling is premised on the following three main criteria: the effort of dedicated individuals; good management; and/or participation by stakeholders. Dedication and commitment are difficult to replicate. At this stage, good management may also be difficult to replicate in the public sector, though as part of the devolution plan, this should be a medium-term goal. In the short-term, again as part of the devolution plan, the main effort should be directed at making the SMCs/PTAs truly empowered so that stakeholder interest for good schooling is harnessed.

Successful participation requires that parents and community members have an incentive to participate, are adequately mobilized and trained, and are effectively empowered so that teachers have a reason to respond to their suggestions. However, for this reform to work, teachers also need to be adequately motivated. While government sector teachers are paid much better than non-government sector teachers, the quality of individuals drawn into teaching will remain poor as long as they are paid less than even half the salary of skilled workers.

The SMCs/PTAs' monitoring should include absenteeism by students and teachers. They would also need to find ways to curb dropout rates and encourage enrollments via incentives such as fee waivers and free or subsidized uniforms, school supplies and books. While some of the good management functions will have to be internalized in the schools via effective SMCs/PTAs, other good management functions like regular in-service teacher training and capacity building, lesson plan and teacher monthly report reviews, monitoring and evaluation, data collection, standard setting and audits would have to be embodied in trained district and sub-district education officials.

We turn now to the importance of education and on speculating why Pakistan continues to do so poorly. While decision-makers in Pakistan over the decades seem to have realized the importance of education, this has not gone much beyond lip service and the formation of commissions. As the introduction documented, Pakistan is now the only South Asian country rated as low in human development and the main reason for this is low educational attainment. Pakistan's GDP index still exceeds that of Bangladesh and Nepal, but it rates much lower on the education index. Nepal and Bangladesh have an education index of 0.50 and 0.45 (1 being the maximum) compared to 0.40 for Pakistan.

Pakistan has traditionally compared itself to India that now has an education index of 0.59, and a GDP index of 0.55 compared to 0.49 for Pakistan.[1] The human development index trends, made consistent for comparison, show a steady widening of the gap between Pakistan and India from 0.065 in 1975 to 0.098 in 2002.[2] Higher educational achievement has no doubt played a role in this increasing gap, even though in a broader international context India's achievement in this regard has also not been stellar.

There is consensus that education is a key element in attaining economic growth. Using an endogenous growth theory model that became popular in the academic literature in the 1990s, Rodrik (1994, p. 22) showed that about 90 per cent of the growth of the higher performing Asian economies (Korea, Taiwan, Malaysia, and Thailand) could be accounted for by the exceptionally high levels of primary school enrollment and equality in 1960, the base period. Judging from this result, given the current level of educational achievement, one would expect Bangladesh and Nepal to overtake Pakistan in the GDP index sooner rather than later.

Equality was identified above as the other 'initial condition' in the base period that can contribute to high future growth. The concentration of economic and political power results in inequality and Pakistan has historically fared badly in this regard also. In fact, there is also an association between land-based power concentration and schooling. For example, our research in this regard in the mid-1990s showed that big landlords in Pakistan have an adverse impact on village educational attainment.[3] The mechanism for this is likely to be the subversion of school infrastructure for personal use and the desire to keep peasant children subjugated to ensure their entry into a captive labor market. Education can result in enlightenment and self-respect and hence attitudinal changes that are anathema to big landlords. It can also result in migration to cities for seeking economic opportunities and hence a rise in rural wages.

Such 'feudal attitudes' are not likely to be confined to rural areas. Our elites across the board (including the military, civil service, judiciary, and industry) seem to have inherited the snobbish attitude of the British colonial masters if not their work ethic. While there is social mobility and hardworking children of the poor do enter these ranks, the institutional cultures they become part of reinforce negative and self-destructive class attitudes. It is as though what was good for them is not good for the rest partly because the others are not good enough, and partly for fear of competition.

I call these attitudes self-destructive because the evidence clearly shows that as a larger community we sink or swim together. Investing in education not only results in an enlightened population but also a more productive one that enhances profitability and growth. If we are not willing to invest in people because it is the right thing to do, we should do so because it is in our enlightened self-interest.

Power has a bearing on education in other ways also. A fundamental lesson we have learnt in the research for this book is the importance of power in good service delivery and this lesson goes much beyond rural schooling in Pakistan. For example, college professors in the USA are responsive to students because their incentives are structured in a way that they need to be. No doubt there are many conscientious professors who would work hard for the students anyway because that is their moral and professional responsibility. However, others have to be responsive because students evaluate them, and these evaluations are paid attention to by the educational administrations. Thus it is not too far fetched to suggest that in the power configuration between parents and teachers, since the latter are delivering a service to the former, parental input into the evaluation of teachers may make a difference. In the same way, since the local educational bureaucracy is partly there to facilitate teachers in delivering a service, teacher input in their evaluation would change this power equation in a positive way.

Finally, the book ends on the same note it started. The mass communication strategy implicitly utilized in Pakistan to promote education has been based on the human capital model (chapter 4) suggesting a higher economic return to individuals from acquiring higher levels of education. Due to labor market imperfections, this has badly backfired. For Pakistan to achieve universal education we need a mass communications strategy that emphasizes other instrumental (like filling forms and reading newspapers, promoting productivity and economic growth) and non-instrumental (like enlightenment) advantages of education as emphasized in the introduction.

A major problem for public sector basic education is the attitude of recent administrations to the rapid growth of the non-government sector schooling. This growth is being welcomed and essentially viewed as the solution to the failure of the public sector education. According to the Government of Pakistan's Education Sector Reform Strategic Plan (2001–2004), the private (for-profit) sector is to be subsidized. These subsidies should be used instead to ensure quality public sector education since that represents the benchmark for the non-government sector and raising that benchmark would ensure an across the board improvement. Thus what appears to be a pragmatic approach to the problem of inadequate provision and poor quality in the public sector not only subsidizes a 'for-profit' activity, for which there is no justification, but could otherwise be destructive. It also amounts to the state abdicating its constitutional responsibility of providing quality public education; particularly for the poor.

References

Khan, S. R. and R. Siddiqui, 1996/1997, 'Landed Power and Rural Schooling in Pakistan', *Pakistan Journal of Applied Economics*, Vol. 12, No. 2 and Vol. 13, No. 1.

Rodrik, D., 1994, 'King Kong Meets Godzilla: The World Bank and "The East Asian Miracle"', in ed. Albert Fishlow et al. *Miracle or Design? Lessons from the East Asian Experience* (Washington DC.: Overseas Development Council).

UNDP, 2004, *Human Development Report 2004* (New York: Oxford University Press).

NOTES

1. UNDP (2004, p. 141).
2. Ibid., p. 145.
3. Khan and Siddiqui (1996/1997).

Appendix I

Research design, instruments, and sampling

Research design

We collected data based on a small, high-quality sample survey that required extensive fieldwork carried out in the four provinces and a federally administered territory of Pakistan (Punjab, Sindh, Balochistan, the NWFP and the Northern Areas) between September and December 1998. The sampling design was to randomly select NGO schools from available sampling frames, since they are the smallest in number, and to then pick the closest private and NGO schools. To ensure that we were comparing the same level of schooling across NGO, private and government schools, many of the listed NGO schools were excluded since they ran informal schools while the government and private sector schools are mostly formal. In all, forty-three NGO schools were included in the sample and we visited forty-three each of the closest government and private schools.

While, this kind of paired sampling extends the random selection to the paired categories, the final selection of government schools is still an insignificant per cent of total government schools. Thus, while we managed to ensure comparability, the small sample of public sector schools needs to be kept in mind. However, our findings regarding government schools are consistent with other comparative studies with a larger sample of government schools.[1]

The fieldwork involved a total of ten questionnaires or tests. These included questionnaires soliciting information from students, teachers, households and communities. We also administered tests to assess class 3 and 4 students for cognitive skills in mathematics and comprehension and also administered tests to ascertain math and comprehension cognitive skills of the class teacher of class 5. A brief description of the questionnaires and tests follow and the questionnaires are included in Appendix II.

Instruments

Student math tests

This test was formulated by as an amalgamation of the math syllabi of classes 3 and 5, in consultation with other such tests previously formulated. The challenge was to make it a reasonable test for both classes so that it was not too easy for class 5 or too difficult for class 3. The test was in Urdu, and comprised a total of ten sums. All students in class 3 and 5 were asked to attempt it.

Student Urdu/Sindhi tests

This test was also formulated in consultation with the syllabi and other previously formulated tests. The purpose of the test was to ascertain student comprehension. It was again devised to be accessible for students of classes 3 and 5. It comprised two paragraphs and questions based on them. The test included multiple-choice, fill-in-the-blank and short-answer questions. Every student in class 3 and 5 was tested.

Teacher Math Tests

This questionnaire was based on a Matric (O-Level or junior high equivalent) syllabus. All class 5 teachers were asked to attempt the test.

Teacher Urdu/Sindhi tests

This was a comprehension test of multiple choice questions based on a lengthy passage. There were a total of thirty questions. Teachers were given an average of 45 minutes to complete the test and all language (Urdu or Sindhi) teachers of class 5 were asked to attempt it.

Household (student respondents)

This questionnaire was given to all students of class 5. It involved questions relating to family background and household interest in the child's schooling.

Household (parent respondents)

This was administered to the available parent of up to about 15 per cent of randomly selected students in class 5 (with a minimum of five students). This attempted to gauge their interest in education, their knowledge about a school management committee/parent teacher association and their satisfaction with the school. We also used the household visit to generate an index of household wealth.

School facility

This questionnaire solicited detailed information relating to the school and teachers. It dealt with questions such as teachers' training, salaries and absenteeism, number of students enrolled, methods taken to curb student absenteeism, source of funds and problems faced while working in the community.

School management committee

This questionnaire was put to a group of as many members of the school management committee/parent teacher association (if either existed) as possible. The objective was to understand the functioning/ non-functioning of such committees and their impact, if any, in improving the quality of schooling.

Community

This was put to groups of people belonging to areas surrounding the school. The objective of this questionnaire was to gauge the degree of community involvement with the school and to explore community perceptions about the school and how it functioned.

Dropouts

This questionnaire was administered to the parents of students who had dropped out (who had enrolled in class 5 but left the school) and had not enrolled in any other school. It started with the household (parent) questionnaire described above, and in addition attempted to find out the reasons for the student having left this particular school.

Sampling

For the fieldwork, we started with a Society for the Advancement of Education (SAHE) directory of NGOs involved in education.[2] We soon realized this was not exhaustive, since a number of organizations had not been included. To supplement the SAHE directory, we obtained a copy of the Dataline NGO directories (one each for the four provinces and the capital) from the Trust for Volunteer Organizations (TVO).[3] This directory had been compiled in 1991, and included NGOs that had registered by the late 1980s. Those that stated that they were involved in education were sent questionnaires to gauge their current status and involvement in education. This process was time consuming and the responses disappointing. However, we managed to complete this process for Balochistan, NWFP and Sindh.

The information sent back pertained mostly to the smaller NGOs and community-based organizations (CBOs). Since we initially planned to include only the larger multiple-school NGOs in the sample, we began afresh to compile a list of larger NGOs, on the basis of the SAHE directory and the NGO grapevine. Our selection criterion was that the NGO be running formal primary schools (i.e. five years of schooling).

Initially, for financial and linguistic reasons, the study was to be restricted to the Punjab. It was thought that, as the largest province and with the largest number of NGO interventions, the institutional findings from this province would be, by and large, relevant for the rest of the country. After much searching, fifty NGO schools were selected from the Punjab. Because of the difficulty in finding formal schools, even smaller NGOs were included in the sample. Once in the field, we discovered that a substantial amount of the information reported was inaccurate, even though it had been given to us in most cases by the senior management of the organizations in question. The main problem was that many of the primary schools were not holding classes 1-5 as we required.

Because we were not able to find fifty formal NGO schools in the Punjab, we had to expand the scope of the study to include the other provinces. Much of the sampling work had to be carried out on the basis of information received on site, i.e. through various education-related professionals and communities. Substitutions were made when those schools originally in the sample could not be surveyed—generally because the school did not run five classes, was closed due to winter break, was non-existent or too far away from a private school to justify a comparison between the two.

The names and locations of schools finally visited are cited in Appendix I, Tables I-IV. Seven out of the forty-three NGO schools finally included in the sample were of one-school NGOs. For the multiple-school NGOs on the list, we randomly selected about 30 per cent of the schools in the Punjab. When the fieldwork in the Punjab was complete, we continued with random selection in the other provinces to complete the target selection of NGO schools. For the larger multi-school NGOs in the other provinces, the selection ranged from 22 per cent to 55 per cent. Once the NGO schools were selected, we then visited the nearest government and private schools that ran classes up to class 5. Our objective in pursuing this method was to minimize location influences when comparing schools.[4]

Appendix I, Tables 1-4 give an indication of how closely we were able to follow our original sampling plan and detail the NGO school selection process.

By October 10, 1998, we had completed fieldwork in thirteen villages of the Punjab (one NGO school in each village) referred to in Appendix I, Table 1 as phase I. We found that the most substantial section of our sample—the twenty-nine schools being run by the MMBT were non-formal. It was at this stage we realized that sampling fifty schools would require extending the fieldwork to the rest of the provinces of the country.

A rough estimate for a provincial breakdown of these fifty schools that we decided on was as follows:

Punjab	18
Sindh	15
NWFP	10
Balochistan	5

Thus, under phase II of the fieldwork, we visited four more schools in the Punjab as indicated in Appendix I, Table I. After that, we had to search for NGO schools in Sindh, Balochistan and the NWFP. For this, we were able to make use of the questionnaires that had been sent back to us as a result of the mailed survey based on the TVO Dataline Directory (1994). Again, a vast majority of the returned questionnaires for all three provinces (and the capital) indicated that the NGOs involved in education were mostly running non-formal schools. Also, most of these NGOs were running an average of two or three schools.

Appendix I
Table 1: Eligible, sampled, and surveyed NGO schools in the Punjab

Sr. No.	NGO	A	B	Comment	Surveys conducted successfully (Phase I/II)
1	Tameer-e-Millat Foundation	12	5	Random, from list of schools obtained	4 (I) + 2 (II)
2	Hira Taleemi Mansooba	29	10	Random, from list of locations dictated on the phone	4 (I)
3	Sufi Foundation	1	1		1(I)
4	Anjuman Khudaam-e-Rasool Allah	1	1		1(I)
5	Awami Committee for Dev. (ACD)	10	4	Org. found to be existent only on paper – were not able to contact any members at site	0
6	Baagh-e-Rahmat Trust	1	1	School was in urban area	0
7	Malik Maula Bakhsh Memorial Trust (MMBT)	71	29	Random, from list of schools obtained	0
8	Roshni Foundation	1	0	CBO currently handling one ACD school	1 (I)
9	Shuaib Qadria Welfare Society	1	0	Used as on-spot substitute in phase I	1 (I)
10	Qasim Bela Welfare Society	1	0	Used as on-spot substitute in phase I	1 (I)
11	Anjuman-e-Hussain Secondary Association	1	0	Used as on-spot substitute in phase I	1 (I)
12	Anjuman Farogh-e-Taleem	1	0	Used as on-spot substitute in phase I	1 (I)
13	Mohd Yar Memorial Society	1	0	Used as substitute in phase II	1 (II)
	Total	135	50(I) +2(II)		14 (I) + 4 (II)

Notes: A = Total number of eligible schools
         B = Number of original schools sampled

The plan of sampling only NGOs running large networks of schools thus had to be dropped.

The samples selected for Sindh and Balochistan are reported in Appendix I, Table 2 and Appendix 1, Table 3 respectively.

Fieldwork began in Balochistan on 27 November 1999. This meant that schools which were in the winter zone had started to close down for the winter break, which in some areas was eight weeks long. Also, because of the vast size of the province and the scarce roads and other infrastructure, travel was difficult. The sample selected for NWFP is reported in Appendix I, Table 4.

References

Kardar, S., 2001, 'Private Sector in Education', report prepared for the World Bank, Systems (Pvt.) Limited, Lahore.

SAHE (Society for Advancement of Education), 1997, *Directory of NGOs in Education*, Lahore.

TVO (Trust for Voluntary Organizations), 1994, *Directory of NGOs*, Prepared by Dataline Services, Islamabad.

NOTES

1. Refer to Kardar (2001).
2. SAHE (1997).
3. TVO (1994).
4. About three-fourths (96 of the 129) of the schools were co-educational, 18 were all-girl and 15 were all-boy schools.

Appendix I
Table 2: Eligible, sampled, and surveyed NGO schools in the Sindh

Sr. No.	NGO	A	B	Comment	Surveys conducted successfully (Orig/Sub)
1	Thardeep Rural Dev. Prog.	2	2	One selected NGO school was too far from a private school	1 (Orig)
2	Sindh Graduates' Association	9	5	Random selection from list obtained	3 (Orig) + 2 (Nearest Sub)
3	Sindh Education Foundation: Nowa Prabath: Naz Old Boys Association	10	5	All schools turned out to be non-formal	0
4	The Citizen's Foundation	22	7	Some schools didn't have class 5	3 (Orig) + 4 (Out of 16 eli: random Sub)
5	Ahle Bait	2	0	On-spot information	2 (Sub)
	Total	45	19		7 (Orig.) + 8 (Sub.)

Notes: A = Total number of eligible schools
       B = Number of original schools sampled

Appendix I
Table 3: Eligible, sampled, and surveyed NGO schools in Balochistan

Sr. No.	NGO	A	B	Comment	Surveys conducted successfully (Orig./Sub)
1	Helper's Association of Pakistan	3	1	Random selection from list obtained	1 (Orig.)
2	Tanzeem Idarah Bahalai-e-Mutasireen	4	3	1 unsafe area 1 closed for winter	1 (Orig.)
3	Pak. Public Welfare Society	15	0	7 closed for winter 5 too far	1 (Sub.)
4	Tanzeem Welfare Society	1	1	No class 5	0
5	Balochistan Rural Support Programme	2	2	1 handed over to govt. 1 too far	0
	Total	27	9		2 (Orig.) = 1 (Sub.)

Notes: A = Total number of eligible schools
B = Number of original schools sampled

Appendix I
Table 4: Eligible, sampled, and surveyed NGO schools in the NWFP

Sr. No.	NGO	A	B	Comment	Surveys conducted successfully (Orig/Sub)
1	Chinnai Welfare Organization	3	3	Organization found to be non-existent	0
2	Swabi Women's Welfare Society	2	2		2 (Orig.)
3	Swabi Education & Environmental Development Society	3	1	Schools found to be functioning as private for-profit enterprises	0
4	Aga Khan Education Services, Gilgit	23	5	1: no nearby pvt. sch. 3: closed for winter 1: completed	1 (Orig.) 2 (out of 18; random Sub.)
5	Hira Taleemi Mansooba	4	0	On-spot information	2 (nearest Sub.)
	Total	35	11		3 (Orig.) + 4 (Sub.)

Notes: A = Total number of eligible schools
B = Number of original schools sampled

Appendix II

School Facility Questionnaire

*Name of interviewer*_____

*ID Number*_____

*Sr. No.*_____

*Village Name*_____

School Type
    1 = Govt.
    2 = Private
    3 = NGO

School Level
    1 = Primary
    2 = Middle
    3 = High

School Gender
    1 = All-boys
    2 = All-girls
    3 = Mixed

SF1 *Is the class taught as multi-grade or single-grade class?*
    1 = Single
    2 = Multi

SF2 *Does the school run single or multi shifts?*
    1 = Single
    2 = Multi

SF3   *Is there a boundary wall for the school?*
      Note some sort of protection: hedge, barbed wire, etc.
      1 = Yes
      0 = No

SF4   *Is the venue of class 5 conducive to children's learning?*
      Note lighting and ventilation, and then grade.
      (*Worst possible*)   1   2   3   4   5   (*Best possible*)

SF5   *What is the mode of instruction?*
      1 = English
      2 = Urdu
      3 = Mainly English
      4 = Mainly Urdu
      5 = Mainly local language

SF6   *Is mother tongue same as mode of instruction?*
      1 = Yes
      0 = No

SF7   *Are desks available for the students?*
      1 = Yes
      0 = No

SF8   *Are chairs available for the students?*
      1 = Yes
      0 = No

SF9   *Are taats in use?*
      1 = Yes
      0 = No

SF10 *Which of the following are in use?*
      Text books
      1 = Yes
      0 = No
      Note books
      1 = Yes
      0 = No

Pens/pencils etc.
1 = Yes
0 = No

SF11 *Is class 5 being taught indoors or outdoors?*
1 = Indoors
0 = Outdoors   ***If outdoors, go to SF14***

SF12 *If indoors, is electricity available to class 5 in the building?*
1 = Yes
0 = No   ***If No, go to SF14***

SF13 *If **Yes**, are fans available in the classrooms?*
1 = Yes
0 = No

SF14 *Is drinking water available to the students?*
1 = Yes
0 = No

SF15 *Are washrooms available to the students?*
1 = Yes
0 = No   ***If No, go to SF18***

SF16 *If **Yes**, is water available in washrooms to the students?*
1 = Yes
0 = No

SF17 *If **Yes**, are latrines in reasonably clean and usable condition?*
1 = Yes
0 = No

SF18 *Does the school have a bank account?*
1 = Yes
0 = No   ***If No, go to SF20***

SF19 *If **Yes**, who operates it?*
01 = Headmaster
02 = SMC
03 = Community representative
04 = NGO
77 = Others (specify)

SF20 *Is there a deficit?*
    1 = Yes
    0 = No
    2 = Sometimes   ***If No, skip to SF22***

SF21 *If Yes, how is the deficit covered?*
    01 = Ask for community contribution
    02 = Village influential contributes
    03 = Appeal to local politician
    04 = Take a loan
    05 = Leave to government
    06 = NGO
    07 = Owners own funds
    77 = Others (specify)

SF22 *Is there a surplus?*
    1 = Yes
    0 = No
    2 = Sometimes   ***If No, go to SF24***

SF23 *If Yes, what happens to a surplus?*
    01 = School owner gets it
    02 = Maintained in a school bank account
    03 = Belongs to government
    04 = NGO handles it
    77 = Others (specify)

SF24 *Is there a formal billing system?*
    If Yes, *observe*
    1 = Yes
    0 = No

SF25 *What is the school's main source of funding?*
    01 = Fees
    02 = Charitable contributions
    03 = Community as a whole
    04 = Government
    05 = NGO
    06 = Other local donor
    07 = Other foreign donor
    77 = Others (specify)

SF26 *Which of the following facilities are available for the teachers?*
    01 = Blackboard
    02 = Chalk
    03 = Teacher's desk and chair
    04 = Charts/maps
    05 = Models etc.
    77 = Others (specify)

SF27 *Does the school have a library?*
    1 = Yes
    0 = No   *If No, go to SF29*

SF28 *If Yes, rate the quality (1 – 5)*
    (Worst possible) 1 2 3 4 5 *(Best possible)*

SF29 Does the school have a policy to curb student absenteeism? Subjectively analyze. *If you feel some or all of the mentioned measures are taken, tick Yes, else tick No.*

Policies	Yes/No
Talk to students	
Talk to parents	
Talk to them together	
Fine students	
Expel chronic absentees	
Others (specify)	

SF30 *About the class 5 teacher*:

Salary	Academic qualifications	Training obtained	Duration of in-house training	Experience

SF31 *Is there any in-school extra help for weak students?*
    1 = Yes
    0 = No

SF32 *Does class 5 teacher provide tuition after school hours?*
   1 = Yes
   0 = No

SF33 *What impediments do you (the teacher of class 5) face in delivering good schooling?*
   00 = None
   01 = Lack of co-operation from government
   02 = Lack of co-operation from community
   03 = Poor quality and disinterested students
   04 = Lack of good training for teachers
   05 = Confront political and bureaucratic interference
   06 = Teachers arbitrarily transferred
   07 = Supplies not provided
   08 = Maintenance/repair not sanctioned
   77 = Others (specify)

SF34 *Was becoming teacher your first occupational choice?*
   1 = Yes
   0 = No

SF35 *How many days was teacher absent in last working year?*

SF36 *How many class 5 students have dropped out since the beginning of the school year?*

   If zero, go to SF38

SF37 *Drop-out details*:

Student name: Possible reasons:	1:	2:	3:	4:	5:
Parents encouraged dropout					
Schooling too expensive					
School too far					
Education not useful					
Have to help at home					
Have to help at family farm/business					
Parents moved to different community					
Poor teaching					
Harsh punishment/beating					
Teacher absenteeism					
Poor performance					
No single-gender school available					
Poor health					
Expelled					
Other/don't know					

SF38   *What is the school fee charged in class 5?*
___ *per month*

SF39 *Do students of very poor families have to pay fees?*
    1 = Yes
    0 = No   ***If Yes, go to SF41***

SF40 *If **No**, are they simply allowed to attend free?*
    1 = Yes
    0 = No

SF41 *What curriculum do you use?*
    1 = Govt.
    2 = Mostly govt.
    3 = Mostly own   ***If 1 or 2, go to SF43***

SF42 *If not govt., why is that the case?*
    1 = Poor quality
    2 = Too easy
    3 = Too difficult
    7 = Others (specify)

SF43 *Is the school inspected regularly by education authorities?*
    1 = Yes
    0 = No

SF44 *If **Yes**, state how often it was inspected in the last academic year?*
    1
    2
    3
    4

Community Questionnaire

Name of the interviewer _____

*ID Number*_____ *(To be left blank by the interviewer)*

*Sr. No*_____ *(To be left blank by the interviewer)*

*Village Name*_____

School Type
    1 = Govt.
    2 = Private
    3 = NGO
School Level
    1 = Primary
    2 = Middle
    3 = High

School Gender
    1 = All-Boys
    2 = All-Girls
    3 = Mixed

C1   *Did the community contribute the land for the school?*
    1 = Yes
    0 = No
    2 = Land contributed by community & government
                    If No, go to C3

C2   *If **Yes** (whole or part), specify who made the contribution.*
    01 = One local notable
    02 = Several village notables
    03 = Several local notables & average income community
          members
    04 = Several average income community members
    77 = Others (specify)

C3   *Did the community contribute towards school construction costs?*
    1 = Yes
    0 = No   ***If No, go to C5***

C4   *If **Yes**, specify who made the contribution?*
    01 = One local notable
    02 = Several village notables
    03 = Several local notables & average income community
          members
    04 = Several average income community members
    77 = Others (specify)

C5   *Does the community contribute towards the recurrent expenditures of the school (such as teachers' salaries, school supplies, etc.), apart from the fees?*
    1 = Yes
    0 = No   ***If No, go to C8***

C6 *Specify duration of these contributions.*
01 = All make contributions when asked
02 = Parents make contributions when asked
03 = All make regular contributions
04 = Parents make regular contributions
05 = Parents pay school fees as a part of these contributions
06 = Notables make grants to defray these expenses
77 = Others (specify)

C7 *Specify the nature of the contribution.*
Utility bills (e.g. electricity, phone)
1 = Yes
0 = No

Teachers' salaries
1 = Yes
0 = No

Regular supplies (e.g. chalk)
1 = Yes
0 = No

Fixed supplies (e.g. desks, fans)
1 = Yes
0 = No

C8 *Who takes care of routine maintenance work?*
01 = Do it ourselves
02 = Employ someone to do it
03 = Leave it to the SMC
04 = Leave it to the school administration
05 = Leave it to a local notable
06 = Leave it to the government

C9 *Has the community ever had to deal with a major repair?*
1 = Yes
0 = No   *If No, go to C11*

C10   *If Yes, how was this handled?*
    01 = Did it ourselves
    02 = Employed someone to do it
    03 = Left it to the SMC
    04 = Left it to the school administration
    05 = Left it to a local notable
    06 = Left it to the government
    77 = Others (specify)

C11   *Are there any collective efforts being made to enroll eligible children not in school at the moment?*
    1 = Yes
    0 = No   *If No, end*

C12   *If Yes, what is being done?*

School Management Committee

Name of the interviewer _____

*ID Number*_____ *(To be left blank by the interviewer)*

*Sr. No*_____ *(To be left blank by the interviewer)*

*Village Name*_____

School Type
    1 = Govt.
    2 = Private
    3 = NGO
School Level
    1 = Primary
    2 = Middle
    3 = High
School Gender
    1 = All-Boys
    2 = All-Girls
    3 = Mixed

SMC1   *How is the school managed?*
    1 = SMC
    2 = Purely school admin.
    3 = Parents & school admin.
    4 = NGO
    5 = NGO & school admin.
    7 = Other   **If SMC1 is not equal to 1, end.**

SMC2   *Who's idea was it to form the committee?*
    01 = Community members
    02 = Notables
    03 = Comm. members & notables
    04 = School admin.
    05 = Donor
    06 = NGO
    07 = Govt.
    Other = 77

SMC3   *What is the total number of committee members?*

SMC4   *List composition of SMC members.*
    1 = Teachers
    2 = Parents
    3 = Other committee members
    4 = NGO rep.
    5 = Govt. rep.
    7 = Other

SMC5   *Representation of parents on the committee was determined by which of the following?*
    1 = Consensus of community
    2 = Notables
    3 = NGO rep.
    4 = Govt. rep.
    5 = Teachers
    6 = Voluntary action
    7 = Other

SMC6   *Who is the most influential on the SMC?*
     1 = Teachers
     2 = Parents
     3 = Other committee members
     4 = NGO rep.
     5 = Govt. rep.
     7 = Other

SMC7   *Do others get some say in the making of decisions? [ask e.g., before noting answer]*
     1 = Yes
     0 = No

SMC8   *Have there been any conflicts within the committee?*
     1 = Yes
     0 = No   **If No, go to SMC10**

SMC9   *If **Yes**, Specify. PROBE.*

SMC10 *Have there been any conflicts between SMC and Community?*
     1 = Yes
     0 = No   **If No, go to SMC12**

SMC11 *If **Yes**, Specify. PROBE.*

SMC12 *How often does the committee meet?*
     1 = Every week
     2 = Every 2 weeks
     3 = Every month
     4 = Every 2 months
     7 = Other

SMC13 *Do parents leave the committee once their children are not in school?*
     1 = Yes
     0 = No

SMC14 *Has the School admin./NGO/Govt. provided any assistance (e.g. training) for the efficient management of the school?*
     1 = Yes
     0 = No   **If No, go to SMC16**

SMC15 *If Yes, has this been valuable to the efficient management of the SMC?*
    1 = Yes
    0 = No

SMC16 *Cite the main functions of the SMC*
    Ensure teacher attendance
    1 = Yes
    0 = No
    Ensure student attendance
    1 = Yes
    0 = No
    Ensure student discipline
    1 = Yes
    0 = No
    Ensure prompt fee payment
    1 = Yes
    0 = No
    Ensure proper school maintenance
    1 = Yes
    0 = No
    Ensure adequate teaching materials and supplies
    1 = Yes
    0 = No
    Generally ensure good quality schooling
    1 = Yes
    0 = No
    Other = 7

SMC17 *Is late payment of fee a big problem?*
    1 = Yes
    0 = No

SMC18 *Is teacher absenteeism a big problem in the school?*
    1 = Yes
    0 = No   *If No, go to SMC 22*

SMC19 *If Yes, has the SMC tried to tackle it?*
    1 = Yes
    0 = No   *If No, go to SMC 22*

SMC20 *If Yes, specify*
    1 = Talked to teachers
    2 = Approached teachers through relatives in the community
    3 = Reported the issue to the teachers' authorities
    7 = Other

SMC21 *Have these measures worked in curbing teacher absenteeism?*
    1 = Yes
    0 = No

SMC22 *Is student absenteeism a big problem in the school?*
    1 = Yes
    0 = No   **If No, go to SMC 26**

SMC23 *If Yes, has the SMC tried to tackle it?*
    1 = Yes
    0 = No   **If No, go to SMC 26**

SMC24 *If Yes, specify*
    1 = Talked to students
    2 = Approached relatives of the students
    3 = Called for official action from the school against the students
    7 = Other

SMC25 *Have these measures worked in curbing student absenteeism?*
    1 = Yes
    0 = No

SMC26 *What are the major obstacles faced by the SMC in the conduct of its responsibilities?*
    1 = Lack of coop. from parents
    2 = Lack of coop. from teachers
    3 = Lack of coop. from govt.
    4 = Lack of coop. from community
    5 = Lack of funds
    7 = Other

SMC27 *Rate how well do you think the SMC is doing in managing the school.*
1 = Poor
2 = Fair
3 = Good
4 = Very Good

Student Questionnaire

*Name of interviewer*_____

*School type*_____

*School name*_____

*Area code*_____

*Student name*_____

*Student code*_____

S1 *Level of education of father*:
Illiterate _____
Primary _____
Middle _____
Matriculation _____
Intermediate (FA etc.) _____
Graduate (BA etc.) _____
Postgraduate (MA etc.) _____
Not certain _____

S2 *Is the father alive?*
Yes = 1
No = 0 **If No, Skip to S4**

S3 *Does the father work?*
Yes = 1
No = 0

S4   *Level of education of mother*:
Illiterate   _____
Primary   _____
Middle   _____
Matriculation   _____
Intermediate (FA etc.)   _____
Graduate (BA etc.)   _____
Postgraduate (MA etc.)   _____
Not certain   _____

S5   *Total number of adults in the house (excluding parents) who have been to school*:

_____

S6   *Which of the following are present in your house?*
Radio/cassette player   = 1
TV   = 2
Fridge   = 3
VCR   = 4
None   = 0

S7   *Which mode of transport does your family own?*
Bicycle   = 1
Tonga   = 2
Public transport   = 3
Motorcycle   = 4
Taxi   = 5
Personal car   = 6

S8 *Number of children less than 18 years*

	Self	Child 1	Child 2	Child 3	Child 4	Child 5	Child 6
Gender							
Age							
Currently attending school							
Highest class completed							

S9 *Are you assigned homework?*
    Yes   = 1
    No   = 0   ***If No, go to F15***

S10 *If **Yes**, is your homework checked regularly in school?*
           Yes   = 1
           No   = 0
           Don't know   = 2

S11 *Do your parents check your homework?*
    Yes   = 1
    No   = 0   ***If Yes, go to F14***

S12 *If **No**, does someone else check your homework?*
    Yes   = 1
    No   = 0

S13 *Do you generally complete your homework?*
    Yes   = 1
    No   = 0   ***If Yes, go to F16***

S14 *If **No**, are you punished for not doing it?*
    Yes   = 1
    No   = 0   ***If No, go to F17***

S15 *If **Yes**, how are you punished?*
Scolded = 01
Made to do extra homework = 02
Made to stay after school to do homework = 03
Beaten = 04
Other = 77

S16 *How frequent are school tests/exams?*
Weekly = 01
Monthly = 02
End of term = 03
End of school year = 04

S17 *Are you required to show your parents/other elders your report card?*
Yes   = 1
No   = 0   ***If No, go to F20***

S18 *If **Yes**, are they required to sign the report card?*
Yes   = 1
No   = 0

S19 *Are you repeating this class?*
Yes   = 1
No   = 0   ***If library exists***

S20 *Do you use school library?*
Frequently   = 1
Sometime   = 2
Not at all   = 3

S21 *Are you receiving tuition after school or on holidays?*
Yes   = 1
No   = 0

S22 *Have you ever been punished for misbehaving in class?*
Yes   = 1
No   = 0   ***If No, go to F23***

S23 *If Yes, how were you punished?*
    Scolded = 01
    Made to stay after school = 02
    Beaten = 03
    Other = 77

    Refer to attendance register for each student
S24 Attendance for 1st term (April to June '98)

Total no. of school days	Number of days attended	Number of days absent

Family Questionnaire

Name of the interviewer _____

*ID Number*_____ *(To be left blank by the interviewer)*

*Sr. No*_____ *(To be left blank by the interviewer)*

*Village Name*_____

School Type
    1 = Govt.
    2 = Private
    3 = NGO
School Level
    1 = Primary
    2 = Middle
    3 = High
School Gender
    1 = All-Boys
    2 = All-Girls
    3 = Mixed

F1 *Does the school have an SMC?*
    Yes   = 1
    No   = 0
    Don't know   = 2   **If No or Don't know, go to F12**

F2 *Do you think the SMC has any impact on improving the quality*
    of education of your children?
    Yes   = 1
    No   = 0
    Don't know   = 2   **If Yes or Don't know, go to F4**

F3 *If No, state why*
    Meetings not systematic or organized
    Parents decisions ignored
    Influentials make all the decisions
    Teachers make all the decisions
    Committee non-functional
    Other

F4 *If Yes, are you or any other member of your family a member of*
    the SMC?
    Yes   = 1
    No   = 0
    Don't know   = 2

F5 *How important do you consider education to be for your*
    children?
    Very important
    Of some importance
    Not important

F6 *Have you (or your spouse) ever discussed your children's*
    education with their teachers?
    Yes   = 1
    No   = 0
    Don't know   = 2   **If No, or Don't know, go to F8**

F7   *If **Yes**, have you or your spouse ever initiated any of these meetings?*
Yes   = 1
No   = 0
Don't know   = 2

F8   *How often do these discussions occur?*
Regularly   = 1
As needed   = 2
Don't know   = 3

F9   *Does your child receive homework from school?*
Yes   = 1
No   = 0
Don't know   = 2   **If No or Don't know, go to F11**

F10 *If **Yes**, do you or a member of your family help your child with his/her homework?*
Yes   = 1
No   = 0
Don't know   = 2

F11 *Does your child receive paid tuition?*
Yes   = 1
No   = 0
Don't know   = 2

F12 *Do you or any other member of your family remind your child to do his/her homework?*
Yes   = 1
No   = 0
Don't know   = 2

F13 *Do you or your spouse think your child faces problems with his/her educational progress?*
Yes   = 1
No   = 0
Don't know   = 2   **If No, or Don't know, go to F16**

F14 *If **Yes**, what is the nature of these problems?*
   Read badly   = 1
   Can't write well   = 2
   Can't solve basic problems   = 3
   Other   = 4
   Don't know   = 0

F15 *If **Yes** to 14, do you find the teachers responsive?*
   Yes   = 1
   No   = 0
   Don't know   = 2

F16 *Is the child taught in his/her mother tongue?*
   Yes   = 1
   No   = 0
   Don't know   = 2   ***If Yes, go to F18***

F17 *If **No** or **Don't know**, do you think the child should be taught in his/her mother tongue?*
   Yes   = 1
   No   = 0
   Don't know   = 2

F18 *Do you have to migrate during different seasons for work or other reasons?*
   Yes   = 1
   No   = 0   ***If No, go to F20***

F19 *If **Yes**, do you think this disrupts your children's education?*
   Yes   = 1
   No   = 0

   To be observed

F20 *Nature of building of house*
   Katcha
   Pakka
   Katcha-pakka

F21 *Does the house have electricity?*
     Yes   = 1
     No   = 0

Dropout Children & Family Questionnaire

Name of the interviewer _____

*ID Number*_____ *(To be left blank by the interviewer)*

*Sr. No*_____ *(To be left blank by the interviewer)*

*Village Name*_____

*Student Name*_____

School Type
     1 = Govt.
     2 = Private
     3 = NGO
School Level
     1 = Primary
     2 = Middle
     3 = High
School Gender
     1 = All-Boys
     2 = All-Girls
     3 = Mixed

Part I *To be addressed to dropped child:*

D1   *Level of education of father*
        01 = Illiterate
        02 = Less than primary
        03 = Primary
        04 = Middle
        05 = Matriculation
        06 = Intermediate (FA etc.)

07 = Graduate (BA etc.)
08 = Postgraduate (MA etc.)
09 = Not certain

D2   *Is the father alive?*
        1 = Yes
        0 = No   ***If No, go to D4***

D3   *Does the father work?*
        1 = Yes
        0 = No

D4   *Level of education of mother*
        01 = Illiterate
        02 = Less than primary
        03 = Primary
        04 = Middle
        05 = Matriculation
        06 = Intermediate (FA etc.)
        07 = Graduate (BA etc.)
        08 = Postgraduate (MA etc.)
        09 = Not certain

D5   *Does the house have electricity?*
        1 = Yes
        0 = No

D6   *Nature of building of house* (To be observed)
        1 = Katcha
        2 = Pakka
        3 = Katcha-pakka

D7   *Which of the following are present in your house?*
        00 = None
        01 = Radio/cassette player
        02 = Fridge
        03 = TV
        04 = VCR

D8   *Which mode of transport does your family own?*
        00 = None
        01 = Bicycle
        03 = Motorcycle
        04 = Personal car

D9   *Number of children less than 18 years*

	Self	Child 1	Child 2	Child 3	Child 4	Child 5	Child 6
Gender							
Age							
Currently attending school							
Highest class completed							

D10   *Were you repeating the class?*
        1 = Yes
        0 = No

D11   *Did you receive tuition after school or on holidays?*
        1 = Yes
        0 = No

D12   *Were you ever been punished for misbehaving in class?*
        1 = Yes
        0 = No   ***If No, go to D14***

D13   *If **Yes**, how were you punished?*
        01 = Scolded
        02 = Made to stay after school
        03 = Beaten
        77 = Others (Specify)

D14   *Dropout details*

Student name: Possible reasons:	Tick whichever is applicable
Parents encouraged dropout	
Schooling too expensive	
School too far	
Education not useful	
Have to help at home	
Have to help at family farm/business	
Parents moved to different community	
Poor teaching	
Harsh punishment/beating	
Teacher absenteeism	
Poor performance	
No single-gender school available	
Poor health	
Expelled	
Others/don't know	

Part II: To be administered to parent or relevant family head (Family Questionnaire).

Index

Hoxby, C.M., 92
Human Capital Theory, 116
Hussein, M.H., 64, 67

I

International Food Policy Research
    Institute (IFPRI), 118
International Institute of Education, 64

J

Jimenez, E., 64
Jolly, R., 1

K

Khan, S.R., 58, 64
Khidmat (service) committees, 66
Khwendo Kor, 67
King, E.M., 64

L

Levin, H.M., 92

M

Merchant, N., 64, 66
Modern Schools, 35
Monk, D.H., 92

N

National Education Policy, 122
Ninth Plan period, 5
NGO schools: Multi school NGO program,
    33-7; Unsuccessful and successful
    single school NGO, 31
Non-government schooling: Growth, 13
North Public School, 32
NWFP, 61

O

Oh, G., 64
Olson, M., 58
Orazem, P.F., 64
Ozler, B., 64

P

Pakistan Integrated Household Survey
    (PIHS), 2
Pakistan Ministry of Food and Agriculture,
    118
Parent Teacher Association (PTA), 33, 61,
    68-72. *See also* School Management
    Committees (SMCs)
Podgurski, M., 117
Primary Teachers Certificate (PTC), 97
Principal-agent model, 21-3
Private Schools, 29-31
Production Theory: Cognitive Skills, 93
Punjab, 61

R

Randall, L., 64
Raven's Coloured Progressive Matrices
    (CPM), 119

S

Sabot, R., 83
Sawada, Y., 64
Salary Structure, 118-23
School Management Committees (SMCs),
    10, 30, 35, 60-4, 68-72. *See also*
    Parent Teacher Association (PTA)
Sindh, 61
Sindh Education Management Information
    System (SEMIS), 67
Social Action Program (SAP): Objectives,
    7-13; Projects, 1-10, 63
Stewart, F., 1
Stone, J.A., 92
Swabi, 32

Swamy, A., 64

T

Tharparker, 32

U

UNICEF support, 66

V

Village Education Committees (VECs),
    37, 48

W

Wakeman-Linn, J., 83
Whitefield Public School, 35
Winkler, D.R., 64
World Bank, 79-85